Teaching Machines

By DR. BENJAMIN FINE

STERLING PUBLISHING Co., Inc.
New York

DEDICATION

To my wife, Lillian Rose
And our machine-age daughters, Ellen Sydney, Jill Barbara, Carla Coleman, Janet Eva
This book is affectionately dedicated.

PICTURE CREDITS

The publishers wish to thank the following people and organizations for the photographs, drawings and samples which appear in this book:

Basic Systems, Inc., page 61; Doubleday and Co., Inc., page 69; Encyclopaedia Britannica Films, Inc. (and Anna M. Rosenberg Associates), pages 33, 39, 64, 65, 67, 74, 97, 125, 145, 166; Grolier, Inc. (and Teaching Machines, Inc.), pages 18, 40, 84, 108, 156; Harcourt, Brace and World, Inc., page 34; J. Frederick Laval—Photography, pages 25, 29, 31, 51, 59, 82, 113; Point Park Junior College, page 76; Universal Electronics Laboratories Corp., page 32; and U.S. Industries, Inc., pages 30, 36, 122.

Copyright © 1962 by
Bold Face Books, Inc.
Distributed by Sterling Publishing Co., Inc.
419 Fourth Avenue, New York 16, N.Y.
All rights reserved
Manufactured in the United States of America
Library of Congress Catalogue Card. No.: 61-15736

ACKNOWLEDGMENTS

I wish to acknowledge my indebtedness to the many individuals who helped me discover the story of the teaching machine movement. It would be impossible to name the host of teachers, psychologists, administrators, students and parents whom I interviewed during the past year, and who gave me invaluable insight and inspiration. To all of these cooperative assistants I am grateful.

I would be remiss, though, if I did not specifically thank the following individuals by name, for the important help they gave me: Genevieve Bell, Point Park Junior College, Pittsburgh, Pa.; Allen D. Colvin, psychologist, Encyclopaedia Britannica Films; Dr. James E. Evans, and Dr. Lloyd Homme of Teaching Machines, Incorporated, Albuquerque, N.M.; Dr. Robert Glaser, psychologist, University of Pittsburgh; Thomas Rosenberg, Anna M. Rosenberg Associates, New York City; Dr. David G. Salten, Superintendent of Schools, Long Beach, New York; Theodore Waller, President, Teaching Materials Corporation, New York City. I wish to thank William A. Platt for his editorial assistance. Also, my appreciation to Jeff Stansbury and Kazu Iijima.

Above all, I want to express my appreciation to my wife, Lillian, for her patience and sympathetic understanding, even though as a high school teacher of English her natural inclination might well be symbolized by the cheerful red apple rather than the foreboding oil can.

Table of Contents

CHAPTER I

An Oilcan for the Teacher   PAGE 19

This is a book about teaching machines. The .... is a device that helps the student learn faster and in a different way.
    1.1

1.1
teaching
machine

The teaching machine permits the learner to go at his own pace. Because a person can go at his own .... he can learn by himself and learn ......, too.
    1.2

1.2
pace
faster

The teaching machine is a ......-teacher, and encourages the learner to work harder.
    1.3

5

1.3
self

I describe some of my interviews with students and teachers in this chapter. The shiny red apple will not be replaced by the ..... as a symbol.

1.4

CHAPTER II

PAGE
What Is a Teaching Machine?   27

1.4
oilcan

A teaching machine is a ....-..... device. It is based generally on the psychological findings of Dr. B. F. Skinner of Harvard.

2.1

2.1
self-teaching

But the teaching machine is not only a machine. It is also possible to get the same principles from a programmed book. It is what goes into the pages of the ...... that is important.

2.2

2.2
book

There are different types of ....
They sell from $20 each to $5,000.

2.3

2.3
teaching
machines

The major difference in the type is that the ..... machines are operated manually, while the expensive ones are operated electronically.

2.4

6

2.4
cheaper

Experiments show that there is little .... between a "hardware" type of teaching machine and the ...... type of teaching machine.

2.5

2.5
difference
book

Research shows that
a) machines are better than books.
b) books are more popular.
c) more research is needed.
        yes... no... (on each).

2.6

2.6
a) not proved
b) yes
c) yes

The books used are not very different from ordinary books. You're talking about a strange kind of text, that's all.
a) there really is no difference.
b) the principles are entirely different.
c) you can use either new or old texts.

2.7

2.7
a) how wrong you are
b) correct
c) of course you can't

But what is the difference between books and machines? You say the principles are the same.
a) the difference is in the cost of program.
b) machines are a novelty, and keep students' attention longer.
c) both books and machines depend upon programmed instruction to do an adequate job.

2.8

7

CHAPTER III

Programmed Learning   PAGE 45

2.8
a) not the real difference
b) could be, but that's irrelevant
c) correct; it's what goes into machine that counts

Programmed learning is a new technique that may revolutionize teaching methods. The basic principle of .... is that students learn in small sequential steps.

3.1

3.1
programmed learning

One important principle is that the lessons are so arranged as to minimize the number of errors made by the student. By avoiding ..... the student enjoys his studies.

3.2

3.2
errors

Another basic principle is that of reinforcement. As soon as a student puts down his answer to a question in the ..... course, he knows whether he is right or .....

3.3

3.3
programmed
wrong

Dr. Skinner found, through experiments with pigeons, that he could get them to do complex acts by .... them with kernels of corn. He broke up the ..... steps into tiny simple ones.

3.4

8

3.4
rewarding
(reinforcing)
complex

Students that I interviewed said they liked p...... l..... They liked going at their own ...... Many finished a six-month course in ..... the time of an ordinary course.

3.5

CHAPTER IV

How Do Students Respond?

PAGE
71

3.5
programmed learning
pace
half

Some people might worry that t..... m.... and p..... l.... might make children into robots. I found that this is needless worry. The new techniques did not make ..... out of the children.

4.1

4.1
teaching machines
programmed learning
robots

All types of children benefited from this new .... Bright students finished their programs in ...... the time. The dull ones took longer, but they were happy and they improved the quality of their work.

4.2

4.2
technique
half

The students liked the fact that they knew at once their correct ...... This reward, or ...., stimulated them to do better work.

4.3

4.3
answers
reinforcement

But the children felt that the human ..... was important, too. Lou Ellen (she's 5) said, "... the .... doesn't talk!"

4.4

9

4.4
teacher
But
teaching machine

On the whole, though, programmed instruction has tremendous potentialities to improve American ....

4.5

CHAPTER V

How Do Teachers React?

PAGE
102

4.5
education

The new techniques will not succeed unless the teachers cooperate. Some ...... object to ..... machines because they believe it will take their jobs away.

5.1

5.1
teachers
teaching

On the other hand, the National Education Association and other major teaching groups believe that .... can help create greater opportunities for ...... They say it can help get rid of teaching drudgery.

5.2

5.2
programmed instruction
teachers

A machine will never replace a ....., almost everyone agrees. But the .... can help improve instruction and make .... more exciting.

5.3

10

5.3
teacher
teaching
machine
education
(teaching)

In interviews with ....., I found that one question arose frequently: can the .... really teach? The answer is no. They, by themselves, do not .... What goes into the machines is the ..... factor.

5.4

5.4
teachers
machines
teach
crucial

Those .... who used the new method agreed that the ..... was taken out of teaching. They saw it as a ...... and an academic revolution.

5.5

CHAPTER VI

PAGE

What Can Teaching Machines Teach?   119

5.5
teachers
drudgery
challenge

Many subjects are being taught through .... Math and geometry are the most popular. These are .... subjects, in a sense. It is easier to teach "tool" courses via machines.

6.1

6.1
programmed
instruction
mechanical

Even philosophy, logic and religion have been taught by this new method. Some doubt the advisability of teaching .... subjects by machine.

6.2

11

6.2
creative

Subjects include Russian, statistics, music and many others. New ...... are being added right along. Much more ...... needs to be done to improve programs.

6.3

6.3
subjects
research

All grades, from kindergarten through college are included. ...... children, before they can read, have experimented with ....

6.4

6.4
Kindergarten
teaching
machines

Adult education is a natural ...... for programmed instruction. We can expect growth in home study courses for ......

6.5

6.5
subject
adults

Teaching machines can also be used in underdeveloped countries. These countries lack adequate ..... and cannot afford schools. Machines are less ...... and more ....

6.6

6.6
teachers
expensive
economical

Industry is making good use of .... It saves ..... money in training personnel.

6.7

6.7
programmed
instruction
industry

The military services, in many experiments, have shown that .... is valuable. Complicated subjects such as electronics and mechanics, are made ......

6.8

12

CHAPTER VII

Are Administrators Accepting Machines?

PAGE 139

6.8
programmed
instruction
easy

I made a survey of 300 school superintendents to find out what they thought of .... The overwhelming majority said they planned to .... them on an experimental basis soon.

7.1

7.1
teaching
machines
introduce

A typical response was: "We'll give it a fair trial." They agreed that the .... of teaching machines were sound.

7.2

7.2
psychological
principles

Some superintendents, on the other hand, expressed ...... to teaching machines. They felt this method would extend ..... education problems.

7.3

7.3
opposition
mass

Without exception, the superintendents said that .... would not replace the ..... in the classroom. Machines cannot comfort an unhappy .... nor run a birthday party.

7.4

7.4
programmed
instruction
teacher
child

It is expected that teaching machines will add to the school budget. Board members say that the costs will increase by: *a)* 10 per cent, *b)* 25 per cent, *c)* 50 per cent, *d)* 100 per cent, *e)* no one knows.

7.5

7.5
e) no one knows; it is still too early to tell what installing machines will cost

How much do teaching machines cost? You can get a good machine for *a)* $20, *b)* $100, *c)* $1,000, *d)* $5,000.

7.6

7.6
a) $20, the Min-Max

In the long run, teaching machines will be cheaper than traditional learning methods because students will get better education in less time. yes..... no....

7.7

7.7
yes

Quality can be improved through teaching machines, because the student *a)* gets reinforcement, *b)* is able to cheat, *c)* must stay with rest of class, *d)* is not allowed to take machines home.

7.8

7.8
a) gets reinforcement

On the whole, based on views of leading educators, the future of .... looks good. Education will be stronger and better in the long run if teachers ...... this program.

7.9

14

CHAPTER VIII

Challenges Ahead
PAGE 152

7.9
programmed
instruction
accept
(adopt, approve)

Many problems lie ahead for ....-.... education. Much more ...... needs to be done.

8.1

8.1
teaching-
machine
experimentation

Not all students will benefit from this .... Some pupils and teachers are ...... of machines.

8.2

8.2
instruction
afraid

Cultural ..... may stop the machine this time just as it did in the 1920's when Prof. ..... of Ohio University invented the first machine.

8.3

8.3
inertia
Pressey

Many bugs have to be straightened out. Uniformity is needed in ...... and range of ...... to be taught.

8.4

8.4
programs
subjects

Teaching machines can break the .... of education by permitting more children to have ...... education.

8.5

15

8.5
lock step
individual

Drastic changes may take place in .... because the regular classroom set-up may no longer be needed.

8.6

8.6
schools

With a teacher .... and a building ..... the machines may be able to circumvent these shortages and provide better ..... as well.

8.7

8.7
shortage
shortage
quality

Programmed instruction can help reduce the ...... rate in underdeveloped countries.

8.8

8.8
illiteracy

Tremendous opportunities lie ahead. The .... principles involved can ...... American education.

8.9

8.9
psychological
revolutionize

With further ..... it can be shown whether the .... will alter American education and provide better .... of instructions.

8.10

8.10
experimentation
teaching
machine
quality

The teaching machine will influence and affect our lives for years to come. Nothing as significant has come to this country since John Dewey's .... system.

8.11

16

CHAPTER IX

Research Findings   PAGE
                                           167

8.11
progressive
education

Many experiments are underway in schools, colleges and industry. These experiments have shown that the teaching machine can be used outside the schools ....
                 yes... no...

9.1

9.1
yes

The experiments have received wide scale support from Ford, Carnegie and U.S. Office of Education.
                 yes... no...

9.2

9.2
yes

More experimentation is unnecessary because we have the answers we need right now. Anything else would be extravagant research.
                 yes... no...

9.3

9.3
no

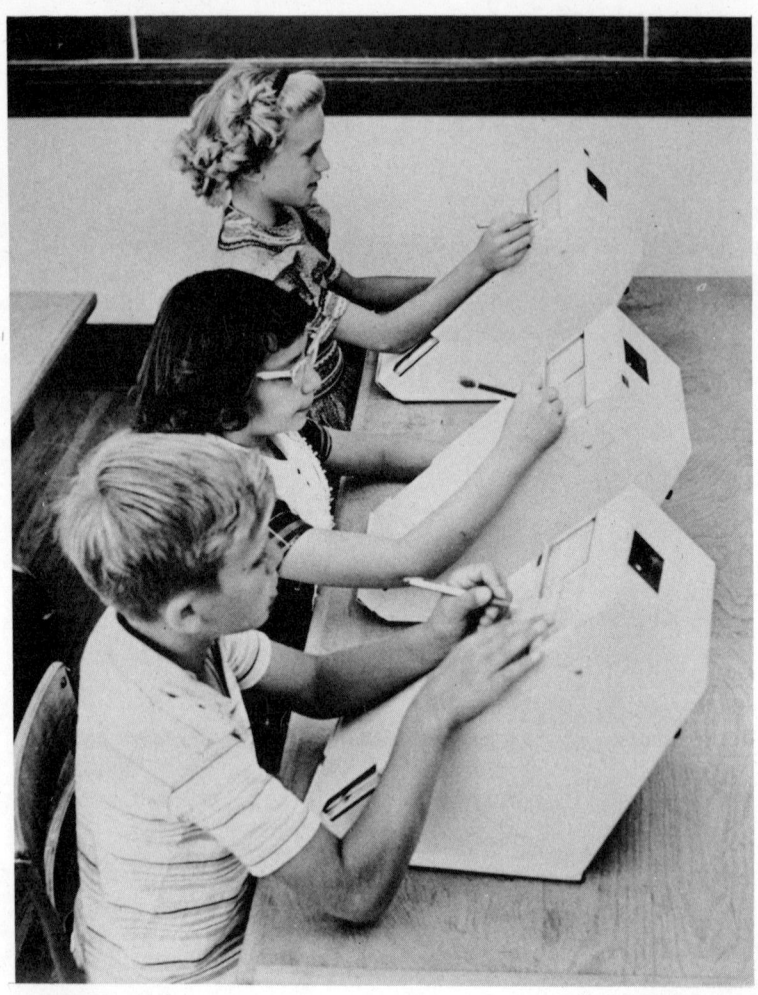

Elementary school students working at their own pace on Min-Max teaching machines into which sheets of paper have been inserted, so that question after question appears in the window. After the student writes his answer in the window, he moves the paper up in the machine and immediately compares his answer with the correct one.

CHAPTER ONE

An Oilcan for the Teacher

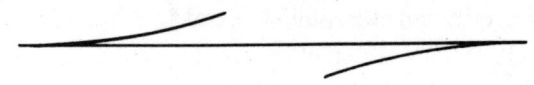

"*Teaching machines and programmed learning are the greatest educational innovations of our time.*"

"*If you don't have a gadget called the teaching machine, don't get one. Don't buy one, don't borrow one, don't steal one. If you have such a gadget, get rid of it. The teaching machine is a disease.*"

There you have what might be called a discord.

Somewhere between the trumpet flourish of Theodore Waller, programmed learning publisher, and the death-march drumbeat of Dr. Thomas F. Gilbert, psychologist, may be heard the true sound of the teaching machine. To my ear one is more nearly on key, but it is really for the reader to decide.

Decide you probably must, for the teaching machine is no mere gimmick of a passing day. Very likely it will be around for a long time, and then, whether you are a parent, student, or teacher, it will leave its imprint on your life.

Why? Because the way we teach our children is of vital

concern to us all, and the teaching machine may be very close to what Mr. Waller says it is.

For the first time in the history of mass education, the machine's *aficianados* argue, the way is open for us to treat each student as he really is: as an individual. No longer must he be forced into one rigid lock step with the rest of his class. If he is exceptionally gifted, we can educate him exceptionally fast. If he is slow, we can educate him slowly and well. Unlike his distant and recent predecessors, the new student will neither be retarded nor pulled ahead too quickly by his schoolmates. The truly wonderful thing is that regardless of his ability, he will learn faster and better than he ever did before.

This achievement has been the hope of educators for decades. How, they have asked, do you educate millions of people in a democracy with precise regard for their individual talents? For decades we simply didn't. Now it looks as if psychologists have found the answer—in the teaching machine.

There are many kinds of teaching machines, even at this early stage of their development, but they all have certain traits in common. Whether they are simple boxes with gears, knobs, and openings for questions and answers, or electronic devices wired for light and sound, or books that look like ordinary textbooks on the outside but can't be read in the ordinary way—they all encourage the student to learn at his own best pace.

Teaching machines are new, even revolutionary, but they use a question-and-answer technique which is thousands of years old. Socrates, who walked the streets of Athens twenty-four centuries ago, was its first advocate. Socrates was a bad politician but a great philosopher and teacher, and his method was very simple. If we accept literally the accounts of his most famous pupil, Socrates never had his students memorize long lists of facts or elaborate ideas. Instead he asked them simple questions.

When they had answered a question, he would say, "Yes, that may be so, but how do you account for such and such?"

Another answer.

"Ah, I see what you mean," he would say, "but does this not then lead to the position that all just men are thieves?"

An irritating, gracious fellow was Socrates, and he made his students think with clarity. They were stimulated, and they learned well.

In the last few years, psychologists have rediscovered the Socratic method and made it the crux of the teaching-machine movement.

Teaching machines are merely devices which contain this new kind of instruction. It is called "programmed instruction," and it teaches by asking questions. In the beginning of a course the questions are simple. Then, by degrees, they grow more complex, although the advance from one question to the next is never too much for a student to grasp. Moving just as fast as his wits can take him, he may finish a course in three weeks, or four months, or perhaps, if he is slow, almost the full year required today.

During my research for this book, I learned that the failing rate in a medical technology class at Point Park Junior College, Pittsburgh, had dropped from twelve to three per cent after teaching machines were introduced. The percentage of A and B students rose from fifty to eighty-five. And the students completed the course in 30 rather than the usual 120 hours!

I also heard about a student named Larry Hill who had been studying geometry in a Roanoke, Virginia, high school. Two weeks after the class started he stood up and asked his teacher: "What'll I do now? I've finished the course."

"Impossible," she exclaimed. "No one finishes a semester of geometry in two weeks."

She was wrong. Learning from a programmed course, Larry had finished the course in about one-tenth of the normal time, and he knew his theorems, axioms, and proofs as well as any of his classmates.

At the same time this record achievement was taking place, a mother went to see the guidance counselor of her son's school in Albuquerque, New Mexico. "Robert is a smart boy," she said. "I'm sure there's nothing mentally wrong with him. But he's thirteen years old and he still can't read."

The counselor sent for Robert, talked with him, and decided that he was indeed intelligent enough to have been reading for years. The fault lay in the way he had been taught. "I'm going to teach you to read a different way," the counselor said. In three weeks Robert was learning to recognize words. In six weeks he was reading well enough to rejoin his classmates in the seventh grade. Overawed, his mother claimed she had witnessed a miracle.

There was nothing miraculous about Robert's recovery, however. He had merely been brought into contact with a wisely programmed teaching machine. Encouraged by his ability to answer the machine's questions, he broke through the psychological roadblocks that had thwarted his natural intelligence for five years.

In the achievements of Robert, of Larry Hill, and of the medical technology class at Point Park Junior College, we see the tremendous promise of the teaching machine. This new device works equally well for the brilliant and the troubled pupil, the student in college and the thirteen-year-old. The education of the millions, in which American democracy has long excelled, can now take account of the individual.

This promise has been recognized by industry as well as educators. Over 100 firms are making the machines and the programs that go into them. The field is big and growing bigger. Programmed instruction can be used in schools, in homes, in adult correspondence courses, in industrial training classes, in the armed forces, and in underdeveloped countries where illiteracy is a major problem. The movement has attracted millions of dollars from the Ford Foundation, the Carnegie Corporation, and the United States Office of Education. None of these organizations is noted for throwing money away on wild schemes.

A device as important as the teaching machine is bound to raise important questions. How, for instance, do teachers react to this mechanical Socrates which may revolutionize their role in the classroom? Does the teaching machine teach better than teachers? What does it teach best, and what worst? Should schools be reorganized to handle it? Can they afford it? What do children say about it? Can it be used in the home? What problems are in store for its manufacturers? And what exactly is programmed instruction?

To get answers to these questions, I made a six-months survey of the teaching-machine movement. I visited schools and colleges in Pittsburgh, Roanoke, Albuquerque, San Jose, New York, and elsewhere. I interviewed parents, teachers, and psychologists and sent questionnaires to 300 school superintendents and state education commissioners. Nearly all the superintendents said they were experimenting with the machines. Some were conducting pilot classes, and many others expected to do so, shortly. Harvard, Carnegie Institute of Technology, Hamilton, Michigan, the University of Pittsburgh, Princeton, Ohio State and Southern California were among the colleges and universities knee-deep in the movement.

My survey revealed that the idea of programmed instruction is generally taking hold. At the same time, it is meeting some resistance and stirring up a few healthy controversies. A number of teachers fear the machines; others see in them a release from classroom drudgery. The range of comment suggests that teaching machines have become the focus of a lively debate.

"I don't want my child pigeon-holed by an I.B.M. Frankenstein," says one parent.

A fourteen-year-old girl, speaking of her teaching machine said: "This is terrific. Even though I was out sick yesterday, I didn't miss a thing. All I have to do is work out a few more frames."

Dr. Roy E. Simpson, California Superintendent of Public Instruction: "Parents are buying teaching machines at an impressive clip. Schools must not be the last to recognize their value."

An eleven-year-old: "Could a machine bandage my knees when I scrape them?"

The most charming example of what a teaching machine can and cannot do is five-year-old Lou Ellen, who will enter first grade way ahead of her classmates in reading ability. She's learning to read on a twenty-dollar machine in Albuquerque. As a test pupil in the teaching machines laboratory, she has been chosen, along with others, to discover if, before a new program is approved, it is sound.

"Looking forward to school?" I asked.

"Oh, yes, I want to go to school," she said quickly. After a brief pause, she asked, "Do you know what I want in school? I want a teacher, not this machine."

"Why do you want a teacher?"

"Because a teacher can talk to you. A machine can't talk."

Lou Ellen has a point. A teaching machine can never replace

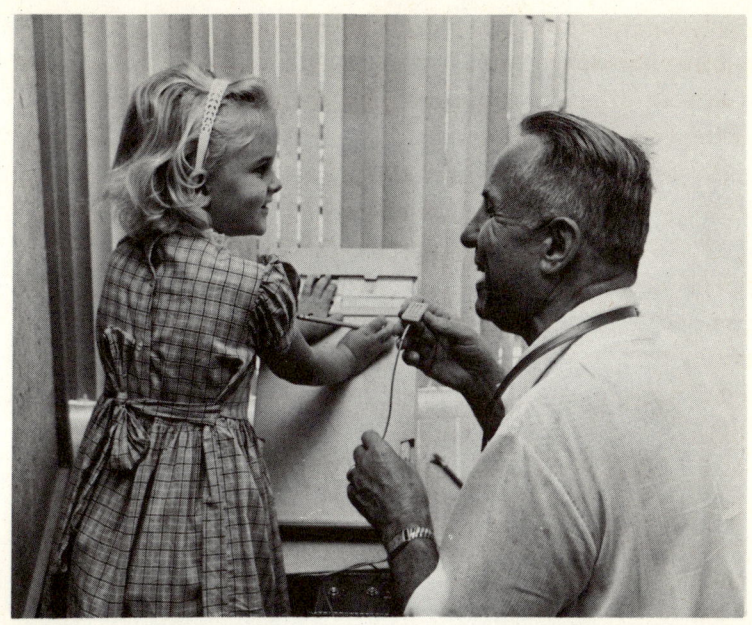

This 5-year-old learned to read on this Min-Max teaching machine. She also enjoyed my interview with her.

the warmth and understanding of a human teacher. A teacher is not just a dispenser of knowledge. She is a source of encouragement and discipline, a storyteller, and an example of the way intelligence works on human character. No teaching machine can duplicate these qualities. But it can be a remarkable spur to learning. Lou Ellen *did* learn how to read on such a machine, and she was far ahead of most children her age. Programmed instruction, limited or not, is here to stay, certainly not as a substitute for the teacher but as an indispensable and powerful ally in the classroom.

How powerful? Early research findings make me optimistic.

I will concede, however, that there is an air of exaggeration to this limerick currently making the rounds of the academic front:
> *The latest word from the Dean*
> *Has come down on the teaching machine*
> *It's that Oedipus Rex*
> *Could have learned about sex*
> *Without even disturbing the Queen.*

The day may not be far off when some student timidly approaches his teacher with a gift. Will it be an apple? No. An oilcan.

Now let's look at some of those important questions.

CHAPTER TWO

What Is a Teaching Machine?

"Hello, I'm your teacher," said the clear voice of the recording machine. "My job is to help you. I free the human teacher for other work. I never get tired or forgetful."

"That's nice," I started to say, forgetting where I was. Then I realized my teaching machine couldn't hear me. I was seated at a desk in a New York college classroom. It was a very unusual sort of desk. There was a record player attached to it, and it also had outlets for a television screen, a tape recorder, and other devices which the human teacher at the head of the class might tell me to use. I had plugged in my earphones, opened my workbook to a course called "Elements of Thermodynamics— Sound and Light," and started the machine.

After the good-natured introduction, my mechanical teacher launched into a seven-minute lecture on the difficult—to me, at any rate—topic of thermodynamics. I had to demonstrate my grasp of the material by answering a series of multiple-choice questions. Here is one of the questions:

"The fundamental forces which are responsible for the

wonders of electronics are (a) electric force and gravitational force, (b) rotational force and magnetic force, (c) none of these, (d) electric force and magnetic force."

With my stylus I poked (a) as the correct answer. A red light flared up on a gadget on my desk and the voice from the recorder spoke pleasantly in my earphones:

"You have chosen the wrong answer. Study your lesson again and then answer the question."

Next time around I poked (b) and my mechanical teacher lost its patience.

"Listen, son," it rasped, "you are being *very* careless. You must study harder. Check with your instructor at once."

By this time I had gone far enough for my research and a little too far for my ego. I gave up. If I had poked the right answer (d) a green light would have flashed on my desk and I would have been allowed to pass on to my next assignment and question.

The machine that flunked me on thermodynamics was only one of many kinds of teaching machines now available to schools. In a way it was unusual; most of the machines I saw asked me to create my own response rather than choose the right answer from a given set. Each system has its own adherents. As we shall see in the next chapter, the debate between them has a great deal of significance.

In Albuquerque I spent several days in the laboratory run by Teaching Machines, Inc., where students were using the inexpensive Min-Max I. The Min-Max is a marvel of simplicity. To ready it for use, you fill it with $8\frac{1}{2}'' \times 11''$ sheets of paper on which questions and answers are printed. The number of pages varies with each subject. In an algebra course there may be over 1,000, while a spelling course may have only 100. The pages are divided into frames. Each frame contains a single unit of

This 6-year-old did not mind my watching him as he learned to read on the Min-Max teaching machine.

information, a question about it, space for a written answer, and a printed correct answer which cannot be seen until the student has made his own response. When the correct answer is moved into view, the student's answer slides behind a plastic screen and thus cannot be changed.

I decided to try a course in Basic Russian. After inserting 40 pages in the machine (enough for an hour's study and testing), I turned the knob and read the information in the first frame.

It said, "The Russian sound, spasebo, means thanks."

The first question was, "The Russian sound, spasebo, means ....". I wrote "Thanks," turned the knob, and looked at the answer. It said, "Thanks."

29

Redeemed from my bout with thermodynamics, I hastened on to the next frame. It said, "The 'a' in spasebo is sounded ah, like the 'a' in father. Therefore the 'a' in spasebo and father is sounded ...." Again I gave the right answer.

The next frame said, "The Russian sound, spasee, means thanks. Fill in what is missing." I wrote, "bo."

Then I came to the last frame on the page. It said, "The 'o' in spasebo is sounded somewhat like the aw in call. Therefore, the bo is sounded ...." I wrote "baw" and once more found I was right. I now knew that "spasebo" was pronounced "spahseebaw" and meant "thanks."

This whole process had taken me less than two minutes. I had answered four questions without a mistake and had thoroughly enjoyed myself while learning a new Russian word. The pleasant quality of my task was no accident; it had been

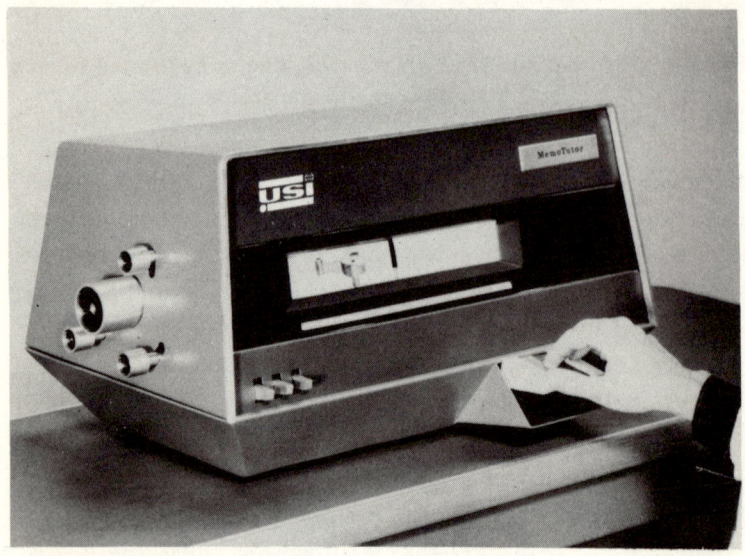

This MemoTutor teaching machine is often used in industry to help in memorizing names of machine parts.

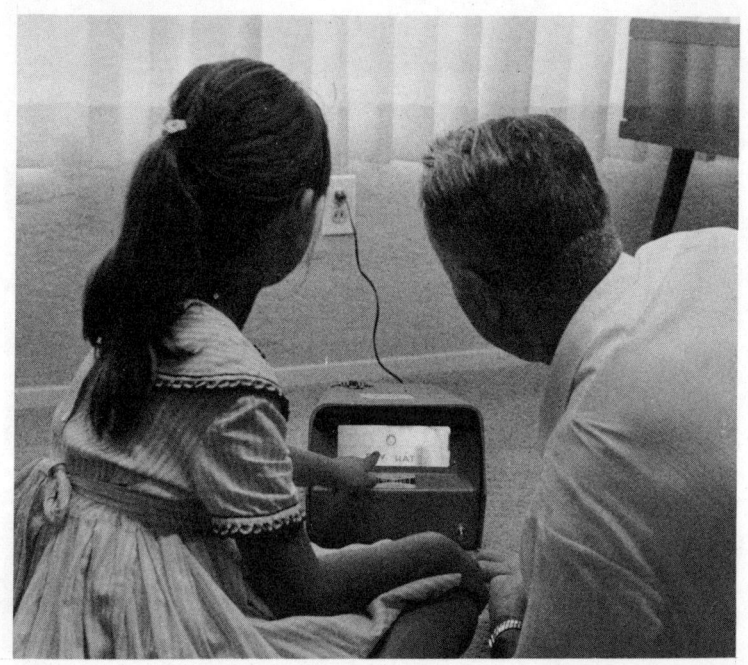

While I watched, this girl had to decide whether the picture on the screen was a boy or hat. She chose the right word, boy.

planned that way by the programmers. Indeed, enjoyable, errorless learning is one of the goals of the teaching-machine movement.

At the present time there are over 100 different teaching machines. They range from the $20 Min-Max machine to a $5,000 Western Auto-Tutor, which uses 35-millimeter film for a program and is operated by push-button. In the middle range is the Astra Auto Score. Its program is printed on $8\frac{1}{2}'' \times 11''$ sheets but works by multiple-choice. The student reads a question, selects an answer, and inserts his stylus in a corresponding hole on the right side of the machine. If his answer is correct,

The Univox machine in use.

the stylus completes an electric circuit and a row of bulbs on the left of the machine lights up.

The machines mentioned so far are different styles of the mechanical type of teaching machine. There is a second distinctly different type: the programmed book. Like most devices and ideas in the teaching-machine movement, it has adherents who are ready to argue its merits at the drop of a conditioned response.

The programmed book looks like a normal text on the outside, but you will never get past page one if you try to read it in the ordinary way. Like the mechanical machines, it gives the student a small unit of information and asks him a question

This student is working on her first year algebra Temac program. The plastic slide at the right covers the answers.

about it. The student constructs his own response, and may check his answer on a following page.

This is the way "English 2600," for example, works. Each page of this grammar by Joseph C. Blumenthal has six frames with answer boxes to their left. Each frame is followed on the next page by a new unit of information, a new question, and space for an answer. The answer to question one is on the left of the frame for question two. A student goes one-by-one through the top frames on all the right-hand pages, checking his answers as he goes, then (starting again in the front of the book) the frames next to the top, and so on until he finishes the bottom frame on the book's last right-hand page. Then he repeats the process with left-hand pages. At this point he has correctly answered every question in the book and has a thorough idea of what grammar is all about. The journey through the text may have taken him two weeks or three months. This sample may clarify the method for you:

raise 1394	Used car prices generally (*rise, raise*) in the spring. 1395	complete 75	A little black dog with big ears . . . Now suppose you were writing a telegram. You might have to reduce this **complete** subject to only one word. Which word would you choose as the most important word in the complete subject — **little, black, dog,** or **ears**? 76
is 1613	Do not use the contraction **There's, Here's,** or **Where's** unless you first look ahead in the sentence and see that a (*singular, plural*) subject is coming. 1614	past 295	Keep repeating these six forms of the linking verb **be** until you remember them: **is, am, are — was, were, been** We say, "I am glad" but "We _____ glad." 296
could 1832	There (*wasn't, was*) scarcely any chicken in my salad. 1833	swam 515	John swam recently. Since the word **recently** gives information about **swam**, we say that it mod_____ the verb **swam**. 516
We 2051	Some of (*we, us*) boys have after-school jobs. 2052	before 735	Lesson **19** Building Good Compound Sentences (Frames 737–777)
prepositional phrases 2270	It takes at least _____ items of the same kind to make a series. 2271	No 955	Grandfather has as much pep as a boy, *who is 76 years old.* To make this sentence sensible, the clause *who is 76 years old* should be put right after the noun _____, which it modifies. 956
babies' 2489	baby babies How would you write that the doctor kept a record of the birthday of only *one* baby? The doctor kept a record of this _____ birthday. 2490 *page 180*	b 1175	The rug was rolled back, *and* then the dancing began. If we removed the conjunction *and*, this would be a (*correct, run-on*) sentence. 1176 *page 181*

Sample pages from "English 2600"

Another kind of programmed text is the scrambled book, which uses multiple-choice questions. The student reads a unit of information on page 37, for example, and then selects one of several answers to the question he is asked. Next to each possible answer is the number of the page he is to consult to find out if he was right. On page 45 he may be congratulated for his brilliance. Page 43, on the other hand, may harangue him for his lack of good sense and direct him to reread the material on page 37.

I tried my wits on a few pages of "Adventures in Algebra," a scrambled (or nonconsecutive) book by Norman A. Crowder and Grace C. Martin. On page 30 I read: "Let us define a symbol. We will say that the symbol n will mean 'any number.' That is all we will say about our symbol n at this time ... Now we will write a statement using our new symbol in accordance with its prescribed definition. The statement is:

$$n=n$$

"Now, bearing in mind the definition we have given for our symbol n, and also that mathematicians are a crabby and cantankerous lot when dealing with definitions, what does our statement $n=n$ say?

"Any number is equal to any number. page 24."

"Any number is equal to itself. page 29."

Well, I knew a little about algebra, so I picked the second answer, which states one of algebra's fundamental concepts. Then I turned to page 29 and read: "This question was a dirty trick, but we went to considerable pains to warn you to be careful. So far all we have said about the symbol n is that it stands for the English phrase 'any number.' Your answer, therefore, is technically incorrect. The trouble is that you are ahead of the argument."

After a few more consoling words, I was advised to return to

I work in math on the AutoTutor with a Crowder scrambled text.

page 30 and try again. This I did, progressing eventually to page 24. Here I learned that while my first answer was temporarily wrong, it would work out fine in the long run.

How did the diverse array of teaching machines begin? These machines have a history. Educators may only now be taking them seriously, but the basic idea of a teaching machine was known and discussed in the United States as early as 1866. The main thing lacking then was scientific knowledge of the learning process, which meant that the machines were not scientifically programmed.

Exactly 50 years ago—in 1912—the famous psychologist, Edward L. Thorndike, in his book "Education," outlined a blueprint for programmed learning devices:

"A human being should not be wasted in doing what forty sheets of paper or two phonographs can do . . . If, by a miracle of mechanical ingenuity, a book could be so arranged that only to him who had done what was directed on page one would page two become visible, and so on, much that now requires personal instruction could be managed by print . . . The improvement of printed directions, statements of facts, exercise books and the like is as important as the improvement of the powers of teachers themselves to diagnose the condition of pupils and to guide their activities by personal means . . . Just because personal teaching is precious and can do what books and apparatus cannot, it should be saved for its peculiar work. The best teacher uses books and appliances as well as his own insight, sympathy and magnetism."

The Pressey Drum Tutor, the first of the mechanical teaching machines, was designed by Professor Sidney L. Pressey of Ohio State University in 1926. About the size of a portable typewriter, its important features were: (1) a window display unit revealing a question with four multiple choices; (2) four keys to indicate your response; and (3) typed sequences of questions (programs) to use in the machine. No change took place in the window when a wrong response key was pressed.

Since the learner had to make the correct response before he could see the next question, a record unit could count all his tries. A modification of the device (in 1927) presented the same question until the learner answered correctly on his first try twice in succession. In the current version of the device (1950) the questions and their multiple alternative answers are presented on a printed page used side by side with the machine.

This early device tested more than taught. But, as Pressey said at the time, there was no reason why a genuine teaching machine could not be built. He thought he might be on the verge of an educational revolution. Unfortunately, he was too far ahead of his contemporaries and in 1932 he abandoned his effort to sell teaching machines to American educators. The statement he wrote at the time was heavy with disappointment:

"With a little money and engineering resources, a great deal could easily be done. The writer has found from bitter experience that one person alone can accomplish relatively little and he is regretfully dropping further work on these problems. But he hopes that enough may have been done to stimulate other workers, that this fascinating field may be developed."

It is now evident that others *were* stimulated by Pressey's work. During the past three decades many psychologists experimented with mechanical teaching aids. The teaching machine itself moved out of their focus, however, as they concentrated on film slides, motion pictures, recording tapes, and television. While these devices were useful, they did not have any impact on the crucial event in all education: the way a student working alone learns something he didn't know before.

It wasn't until the 1950's that this event became the object of scientific investigation. The leading sleuth was B. F. Skinner, a Harvard psychologist who learned about people by studying pigeons. As a result of his work (which we will learn more about in the next chapter), the teaching machine was made ready for its rendezvous with American education.

By early 1962, some 83 different types of teaching machines were already on the market, and the number may soon go beyond 100. These machines were developed by 65 companies, ranging from giant publishing and electronics corporations to individuals working in their home garages. Even more significant is the fact that 630 programmed courses have been prepared for the numerous variations and models that exist.

Summer school students try an E.B.F.-Temac algebra course in Nutley, N.J. high school.

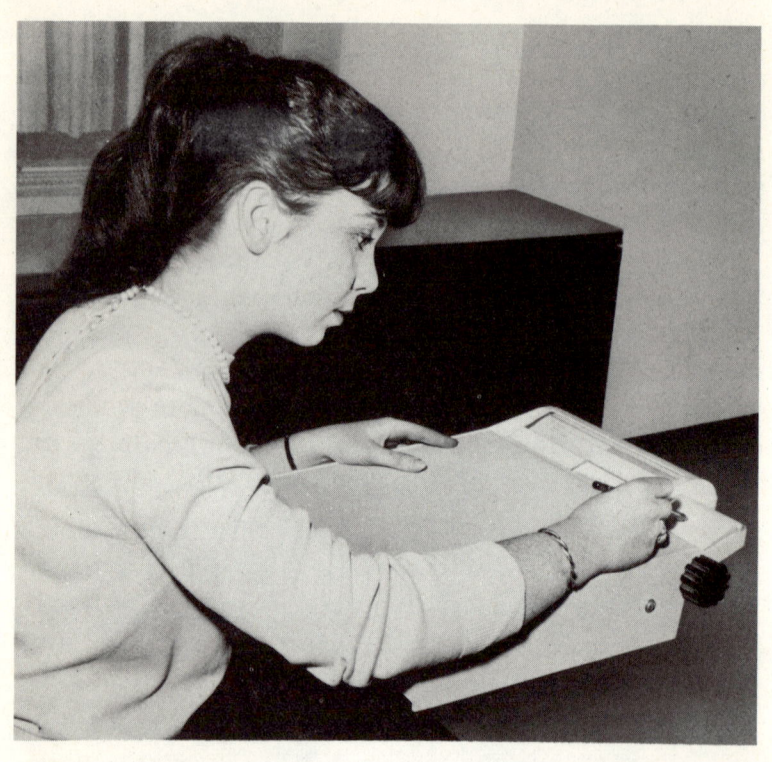

The new Min-Max II has a separate answer tape which makes the programs reusable, and a knob for automatic paper feed of both the program and answer tape.

From this confusion we can extract a few facts. One is that machines using a paper program with constructed or written responses are the most popular.

Many machines are being developed that use complex keyboards, such as typewriter keyboards, alpha-numeric inputs, etc. Some of these are to teach psychomotor skills, such as typing and key-punch operation.

Some classrooms have put in communication systems; these

use mass presentation with individual response. The student presses keys. The teacher then knows the immediate percentile score of the student. She knows how effectively a concept has been taught. The system also helps research and development of programs.

Sounds, words and pictures are used in some of the machines. Frequently the visual portion of a program is put on paper sheets, cards, discs, paper roll, in books, on slides, filmstrips, motion picture film or on computer tapes.

One thing all teaching machines have in common is that they convey information broken down into small, easily digested, errorless segments. How do they operate?

The Grolier TMI Min-Max I, for example, uses a program sheet that a student pushes up with the end of a pencil eraser. The written answers are covered by a clear plastic mask as the correct answer is disclosed. Many children complained that the paper jammed in Min-Max I. This has now been corrected. Min-Max II works on the principle of a knob and roller. The student does not have to push up the paper.

The Atronic Tutor provides its own texts. It gives the right answer only when the correct key is pushed.

The AVTA machine combines a magnetic-tape playback and headphones to provide an audio track, as well as a conventional approach, to teach foreign languages and music.

The Wyckoff Film-Tutor uses filmstrips operated by a button keyboard.

A University of Michigan psychologist, Prof. Harlan L. Lane, has designed a machine that asks a student a question, records his answer, checks it, grades it, and chooses an appropriate next question. And all this at one stroke! Called the Speech Auto-Instructional Device (S.A.I.D.), the machine is primarily useful to teach certain features of speech.

At the University of Illinois, an electronic teacher, called the P.L.A.T.O., can be used to teach any subject from algebra to zoology. It is almost as intelligent as its namesake, the Plato of old. (Actually, P.L.A.T.O. stands for Programmed Logic for Automatic Teaching Operations, not for the ancient Greek philosopher.) Its brain, or central unit, is an electronic computer. The size and speed of its memory determine how many students it can teach at a time. Theoretically, bigger and more rapid machines could handle 500 students at once, each advancing at his own speed. Thus, bright students would move ahead rapidly, and those of average ability would take their time to master their material.

A device for teaching sight vocabulary has been developed at the University of Illinois under a U.S. Office of Education grant, for use with young mentally-retarded children. The machine holds five programmed cards on each of two parallel drums—a cue drum and a response-term drum. The drums are rotated by circuit-control discs. These provide the programmed sequence desired by the teacher. The learner makes his response by pushing one of two switches alongside the display window, on the side next to the response term.

With the large number of machines and programs in the field, how is an unsophisticated user to know which one, if any, to buy? It is difficult. But a joint committee of three national organizations—the American Educational Research Association, the American Psychological Association and the Department of Audio-Visual Instruction of the National Education Association—is now developing standards in both the programming and machine fields.

The term "teaching machine" is alone enough to evoke angry responses in some educators. It contains a built-in obstacle. In some circles the word "machine" is a red flag waved before an outraged bull. Psychologically it is a prejudiced word, carrying emotional undertones. It implies a form of mechanization of the human mind. The Council for Basic Education, for example, is anti-machine oriented. So are many other educational bodies.

Various alternative terms have been suggested, but none has been fully accepted. The term "self-instructional devices" has been used. So has the expression "auto-instructional devices." Others refer to the whole machine movement as "programmed instruction."

I prefer the term "teaching machine." It is succinct. It is short. It tells the story. It is popular. It is challenging and provocative. It is part of our English language. And undoubtedly it will be found in the next revision of the Merriam-Webster unabridged dictionary.

A teaching machine is any device that can present a program. But we know there are many variations, many categories, many types of teaching machines.

Actually, the question is not, what is a teaching machine, but what can it do? What is it designed to accomplish?

Aided by a grant from the United States Office of Education, the National Education Association has set up a technological development project to study teaching machines and programmed instruction. The study, under the direction of Dr. James D. Finn and Donald G. Perrin, although not yet concluded, arrives at this significant conclusion:

"Enough has been uncovered to convince many hard-headed educators that programmed learning and the accompanying devices have a great—some say a revolutionary—potential for education."

The teaching-machine industry has grown so fast that even the experts cannot keep up with it, said Dr. Finn, who is professor of Education at the University of Southern California, and former president of the NEA's Department of Audio-Visual Instruction.

"This is an industry that didn't exist two years ago," said Dr. Finn. "It is a phenomenon that has everyone from stock brokers to school superintendents wondering if they should buy a machine."

The NEA survey lists fifteen functions commonly associated with teaching machines. Seven of these are termed basic, the other eight optional. In the opinion of Dr. Finn, to be called a teaching machine, a device (even this word is a poor one!) must possess at least five of the seven basic functions.

The title of this chapter asked, "What is a teaching machine?" As we have seen, there is no single answer. It can be a metal box operated by hand. It can be an elaborate network of wires and computers with a voice that rasps, "Listen, son, you are being *very* careless." It can be any of several kinds of books. As a matter of fact, the machine itself has only a secondary importance. Much more crucial is the information that goes into the machine. This is called the program, and it represents one of the greatest advances in education since the invention of printing.

CHAPTER THREE

Programmed Learning

If Gertrude Stein had been around when Dr. B. F. Skinner arranged his early tests in programmed learning, she might have thrown up her hands and cried, "Pigeons in the class? Alas!" The first half of that complaint would have been warranted; Dr. Skinner did teach pigeons. But there was no "alas" about it, for in teaching pigeons he learned a great deal about educating the human mind.

Professor Skinner had experimented with pigeons way back during World War II. He developed a program to use pigeons as radar-detecting devices—before radar was invented! Somehow the Army high brass was not impressed. But after the War, Dr. Skinner remembered his pigeons. Could they be conditioned? Pigeons may not be dogs, after all, but if Pavlov could do it . . .

In one of his experiments, he placed a hungry pigeon in a box with transparent sides. Through a hole in the side he fed the pigeon grain or a kernel of corn as a reward for certain desired actions. For example, if Dr. Skinner wanted the bird to turn clockwise in a single, swift movement, he would feed it whenever it accidentally turned its head or took the slightest step in the right direction. After eating, the pigeon would learn to make another clockwise move in expectation of more food. This response-reward pattern would be repeated several times. Then Dr. Skinner would begin withholding grain until the pigeon made a bigger turn. Eventually the bird learned to pivot a full 360 degrees.

Time after time Dr. Skinner found that by first breaking the complex steps into small ones, then immediately and continuously rewarding the birds for successful movements, he could get them to dance a figure-8, distinguish blue cards from white, even play table tennis. He used the word "reinforcing" as synonymous with feeding, since the reward of grain reinforced the learning process.

This remarkably powerful technique has been used to teach pigeons elaborate maneuvers and even subtle color discriminations. In the November 1961 issue of *Scientific American*, Dr. Skinner told how pigeons learned to choose between different colors (or "keys") of light. The experimenter was Herbert S. Terrace of Harvard.

"He programs the behavior in the following way," wrote Dr. Skinner. "When the pigeon pecks a red key for the first time, it is reinforced (fed) and the key is quickly darkened. A dark key differs too much from a red key to evoke a response immediately. The experimenter watches for a suitable opportunity to restore the red color to the key, preferably when the pigeon is turning away from the darkened key. The pigeon at once responds and is reinforced. The darkened key can then be presented for a longer period of time without evoking a response, although restoring the red light brings out a response immediately. Eventually the pigeon responds to a red key and shows no inclination to respond to the dark key no matter how long it remains dark.

"A faint green light is then added to the darkened key. Over a period of time this green light is made more and more intense until it is equal in intensity to the red. Although some pigeons may make an exploratory peck at the bright green key, these responses are quickly extinguished and some pigeons never make such errors at all.

"Terrace has carried the program an important step further. He has been able to teach a pigeon to respond, virtually without error, to a pattern of vertical stripes and not to a pattern of horizontal stripes. These stimuli are much alike and would normally produce considerable generalization—that is to say, a large number of errors—while the discrimination is being established. Terrace begins by establishing the easier discrimination between red and green and then superimposes vertical stripes on the red key and horizontal stripes on the green key. The pigeon responds to the red key with vertical stripes and not to the green key with horizontal stripes. The color is then gradually removed from both keys until only the stripes remain. The pigeon responds correctly to the vertical stripes and has never at any time responded to the horizontal stripes. The experimenter has transferred the discriminative control from one set of stimuli to another through a series of stages so designed as to minimize unwanted responses."

I have quoted Dr. Skinner at some length because he touches on nearly all the germinal ideas of programmed learning and the teaching-machine movement. From his and Terrace's experiments we can draw the following conclusion: The way the pigeons were taught—in very small steps and with immediate rewards after each correct move—enabled them to learn while making few or no errors.

The human mind is infinitely more complex than the mind of a pigeon, but its learning patterns are very much the same. If we view learning as an observable change in behavior we can see the similarity. When a pigeon learns, it behaves in a new way; it starts pecking the red key and stops pecking the dark one. When a human learns, his behavior changes too; he pronounces the Russian word for "thanks" as "spahseebaw" instead of "spaseebow." This kind of change in behavior can be measurably hastened if it is broken down into small steps that minimize the number of false starts or errors. In brief, what works in an experimental laboratory also works for students in a P.S. 83.

"Is the professor trying to make pigeons out of my children?" an irate father asked me, after my interview with Dr. Skinner.

"Not really," I answered. "He's trying to apply the newest principles of teaching to your children and mine."

Our schools complain today of juvenile delinquency, a heavy drop-out rate, school vandalism, apathy, poor discipline, inattention, and a general breakdown in the learning process. Why? Might it not be that the ordinary teaching methods used today are not the best ones? Is the emphasis we place upon marks, grades, diplomas, rank in class, high college-board scores conducive to good education?

Harvard psychologist Skinner carries his analogy with the human race a step further: "A pigeon," he says, "can be made sensitive to the color, shape and size of objects, to pitches, to rhythms, simply by reinforcing it when it responds in some arbitrary way to one set of stimuli and extinguishing responses to all others. The same kind of contingencies or reinforcements are responsible for human discriminative behavior."

Unfortunately these rewards for discriminative behavior are rare in the life of the child. Go into any classroom with 30 or more children. The teacher asks a question. Ten hands go up. One child raises her hand high, waves it desperately, eagerly, searchingly, hoping to be called upon. She knows the answer. She is bursting to tell it. Please, please, her eyes, her hands, her whole body says, please teacher, please, please call on me.

But the teacher does not call on this eager child. She passes her by and calls on a neighbor. Another question. Again the eager child waves her hand frantically. Again she is passed by.

"Why didn't you call on Ellen?" I ask, feeling sorry for the unwanted youngster.

"Oh, Ellen is smart," says Teacher easily. "I know that she knows all the correct answers. I call upon someone who doesn't know."

Later, in the corridor, a sad, frustrated Ellen mutters: "I hate her, I hate her, I hate her. I hate school. She never calls on me. I'm never going to raise my hand in class again."

Be of good cheer, Ellen. Your rescuer, in the shape of a teaching machine, may be on the way to you. When you know the answer, you will not need to raise your hand. The mechanical teacher will call on you automatically and answer you immediately. You won't be frustrated. You won't be left at the starting post. You can go as far and as fast and as eagerly as you wish, and you will say: "I love school, I love it, I love it."

Listen, Ellen, there's more good news. The teaching machine that will serve as your private tutor will also help your live teacher understand you better. Mr. P. Kenneth Komoski, president of the Center for Programed Instruction, found that when teachers learned how to prepare a program for a teaching machine, they became better teachers themselves. The very analysis of methods and approaches improved their skills and techniques.

Mr. Komoski says: "Of course, the idea of individual

instruction has always been the goal of every teacher worthy of the name, and all good teachers are constantly striving to reach the individual child, to encourage him and explain things as clearly as possible.

"However, because of the pressing realities of time and class size, the goal is seldom achieved. Occasionally, exceptional children do work out ways of effectively individualizing instruction, but education as a whole has not been very successful in developing a practical method of bringing this kind of instruction to all students."

Does this mean we will find instant learning on our shelves along with instant coffee, instant potato pancakes and instant tomato soup? No, but we will get more out of education than we have in the past.

Have we found a panacea for all that ails us? No, not a magic wand, but a good right hand, a solid rod and comforter for teachers bedevilled with oversized classes, routine work, bundles of non-professional jobs and tiresome chores.

The Stanford Research Institute in its recent study on "Impacts of a Teaching Machine" said, "Programmed instruction, via a teaching machine, although still in the experimental stage, may well prove a revolutionary route to better quality and lower costs in training and education."

The Stanford educators continued, "The outlook for teaching machines is speculative but highly promising. Although it is too early to predict in detail the manner and extent to which the concept of programmed instruction is to be adopted, it is clear that there are many applications to teaching machines and programmed texts of various types and that the potential markets are both large and diverse."

This view was taken by the conservative Carnegie Corporation in its 1960 annual report: "The programmed learning

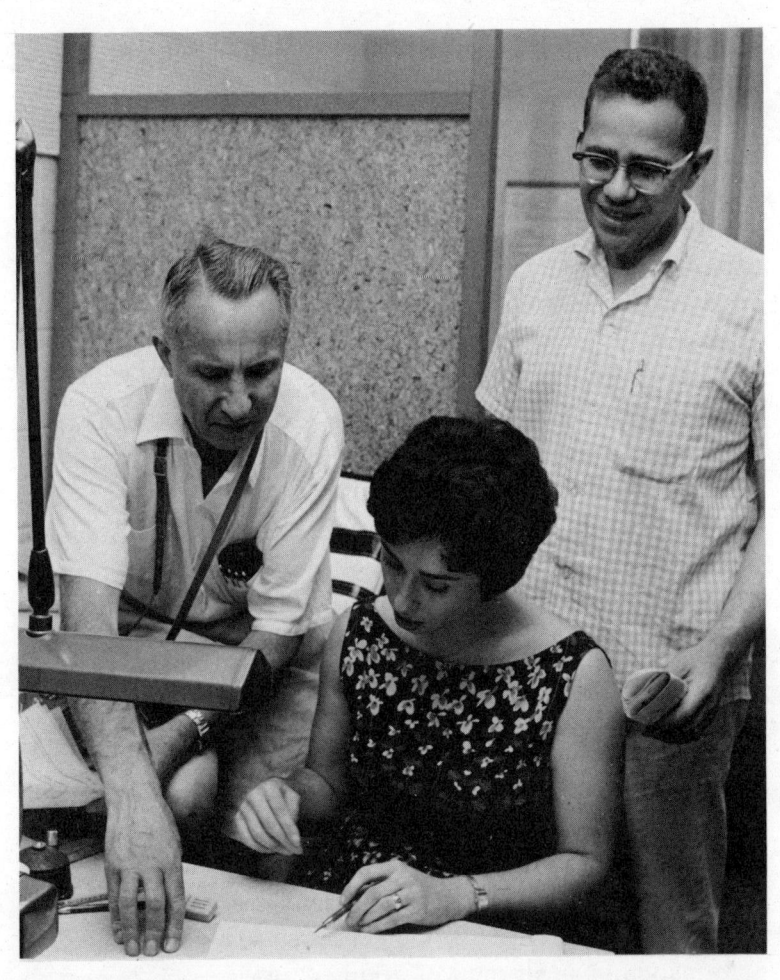

This programmer in Albuquerque is showing Dr. Salten and me how she prepares a program in chemistry.

devices do not represent shortcuts to solve all our educational problems, but they do represent an interesting and significant approach to instruction. They are almost certain to take their place among the important aids to learning in a modern educational system."

The crux of the whole teaching-machine movement is the new psychology of learning which underlies every program inside every machine. According to this psychology, learning is most efficient and more enjoyable when it is programmed into a series of questions and answers.

There are several reasons for this. First, if the logical steps between questions are small, a student will be able to answer any given question correctly on the basis of what he has just learned. Many programs are arranged so that some students may finish a course without a single mistake. There is no better psychological way to encourage a student than to let him discover over and over again that he is right.

Secondly, when a student reads a small unit of information, answers a question about it, and immediately confirms the answer, his new knowledge is quickly imbedded in his mind. This is a much stronger process than the one in which he reads a chapter, takes a test at the end of a week, and waits a day or two longer to find out his grade. The sooner his answers are confirmed, the better is his learning reinforced.

Thirdly, as we have already suggested, the arrangement of information in small steps of "frames" allows each student to take utmost advantage of his own ability. In most classrooms today the slow student is forced to digest the same amount of information in the same amount of time as the fast student. If he wants to keep up with his class, he will have to skip difficult material and leave a muddle of undigested facts behind. He is thus less and less equipped to deal with new subjects as the year progresses. Conversely, the fast student, held in the same lock step, is apt to lose interest because he cannot learn enough. To both of these students who are compromised by the traditional school system with its traditional classroom and traditional textbook, programmed learning is a boon. When learning takes place by question and answer, and when the steps are small, the bright student is encouraged to move quickly. The less brilliant student may advance more slowly, but he is given the chance to comprehend everything he reads and is adequately prepared for new information.

These, then, are the assets of programmed learning: a logical, step-by-step development of material, immediate reinforcement, emphasis on correct answers and a drastic curtailing of errors, sensitivity to individual skill, and active participation by the student in every stage of learning.

It is not enough to dwell on mere techniques, however. What does all this add up to? What basic new feeling will programmed learning bring to the classroom? How will it change the dominant psychology of our classrooms?

Most schools today are dominated by different degrees of aversive control, summed up in the phrase, "You'd better learn or else..." Or else you'll flunk. Or else you'll never go to college. Or else you'll never be a success.

"What can I do about my son? He flunked math," a sad-looking mother asked me. "How will he ever get into college?"

"How old is your son?" I asked.

"He's 7 years old. In the second grade," the worried mother answered. The little boy whose hand she held tightly nervously quivered and quaked.

"Imagine," the mother continued, piercing the boy with a withering look of scorn, "my boy a failure, and he's only 7."

Will the teaching machine eliminate this idiocy? this harassment? this aversiveness? this ungodly fear of failure? this loss of respect for learning?

I once interviewed a teacher who said, "See this paddle? First I try l'arnin'. But if I can't l'arn 'em, I wham 'em." Paddling may be a vanishing extreme, but it symbolizes the negative reinforcements which a student finds in many classrooms today. These reinforcements often stifle his natural urge to learn and rob him of clear motives. If he studies diligently, it is usually to avoid the consequences of not studying: bad grades, failure, the disapproval of teachers and parents. When programmed learning is brought into this kind of emotional climate, the results can be exhilarating. It offers the student not threats but encouragement every step of the way. His intelligence is set to work at its optimum speed and his efforts are rewarded by small but steady gains in competence. Each time he turns to a new frame and finds he has given a correct answer, the discovery is as stimulating as a pat on the back.

"A student using a teaching machine is like a student who has a private tutor to guide him forward, step by step," says Theodore Waller. In brief, the teaching machine makes possible the achievement of two goals that were long mutually exclusive: the democratic ideal of educating a great mass of people, and the Socratic ideal of tutorial instruction.

"Based on what we know today," says Dr. Skinner, "a school system is a failure if it has to use threats to get children to learn. Threats should be replaced by the much more effective techniques of reward and encouragement. Teaching machines have these techniques, in my opinion."

Like the idea of individual instruction, the psychology of rewards is not new; it is merely gaining new respect. Some 2,000 years ago Quintillian advised his fellow teachers: "Do not neglect the individual student. He should be questioned and praised, he should strive for victory, but it must be arranged that he gains it. In this way, let us draw forth his powers with both praise and rewards."

Not long ago the famous educator Frank C. Laubach gave similar counsel in his autobiography, "Thirty Years With The Silent Billion." "We must prove to the student that he can learn easily, quickly, and delightfully, no matter how old he is," Laubach wrote. "Every step must be so short that an ordinary man can take it easily."

This is an almost exact description of what happens when a student works his way through a modern programmed textbook. He reads, he answers a question, and only when he verifies his answer does he proceed to the next item. His attention is constantly involved, his curiosity constantly rewarded. When you walk into a class of students at work on programmed texts or machines, you notice something has changed since your own school and college days. No one is idly doodling with his pencil. No one is staring absently out of the window.

Programs and Programmers

The distinctive quality and rationale of programmed learning has been summed up by Eugene Galanter, a pioneer of teaching machine research at the University of Pennsylvania:

"Programmed instruction is simply a new, better way of writing a textbook," he says. "Our conventional narrative prose is a fine medium for expressing action and emotion, but it is an inefficient way to present information or concepts to be learned. That's why our novels read better than our textbooks. People learn to take in information not from a printed page but by responding to stimuli. Thus, the new textbook begins not with a declarative sentence but with a question. Most of the sentences throughout the book are questions."

What every programmer aims at, then, is a constant engagement of the student in the learning process. When a student reads a page in an ordinary textbook, he is not challenged to respond; he does not know whether he has grasped the information until some later date when it must be dredged up in a quiz or exam. The programmed book or machine forces him to respond. He must stamp every new bit of knowledge with an answer and cannot proceed until he does.

This quality of engagement is only one of many tactics by which programmers hope to strengthen the educational process. I have seen programmers at work on courses for every age group and every kind of teaching device, whether book or machine. They have an interesting task.

To begin with, devising a program requires a great deal of time. Some courses contain as many as 25,000 frames, and occasionally it may take a seasoned programmer an hour to write a single frame. At that rate he would finish a course in ten years. Fortunately, he does not work alone but is supported by a battery of psychologists and experts in his field.

A great deal of work in programming is now being done by Teaching Machines, Inc. in Albuquerque; by Encyclopaedia Britannica Films in Roanoke; by the American Institute of Research in Pittsburgh; and by a group called Basic Systems in New York. On one of my field trips I watched a program for a mathematics course as it took shape in Albuquerque.

The company had deployed its workers into three interlocking cells of activity. One cell was made up of mathematicians who specialized in geometry and were responsible for the hard subject matter of the course; another group consisted of psychologists, referred to as "critics"; the third group consisted of students on whom the new program was to be tested. The students were paid $1.00 an hour to take part in the experiment and were quite excited about both the money and the experiment!

As the program got under way, each mathematician and psychologist was assigned an area of work. Together they arrived at a sequence of facts and questions which they thought would teach geometry in a stimulating fashion. They attempted to write each frame in the program so that it would lead clearly to the next, requiring the student to think about what he had read and make a response which would reinforce his gain in knowledge. On the one hand, they had to avoid asking questions so simple that correct answers would not be rewarding; on the other hand, they followed one of the cardinal rules developed by Dr. Skinner: learning should be as nearly errorless as possible. Wrong answers are like static; they interfere with the clear reception of ideas. Consequently, whenever more than five per cent of the tested students at Albuquerque missed a given question, the mathematicians and psychologists rewrote the frame in which it appeared. (Dr. Genevieve Bell, who developed a medical technology course at Point Park Junior College, was even more meticulous. She reworked her program until its error rate fell to two per cent.)

After watching the labors of mathematicians, psychologists, and students at Albuquerque I asked the company president, Dr. Lloyd Homme, if he thought curriculum experts should have the final say in his algebra program. "I think they should," he answered, " in cooperation with subject matter experts in specifying content. But it's a group effort, and in the end the students must tell us whether the program is good or bad. This is the best indication of how it will work in the classroom."

The final consequence of errorless learning was summed up

for me by Encyclopaedia Britannica Film's Dr. Allen D. Calvin. "When students make mistakes," he said, "we don't blame them, we blame the program."

Some programmers find this role-reversal hard to take. As we shall see later in the chapter, errorless learning is opposed, at least as an all-out proposition, by one of the leading experts in the field. Many teachers have yet to be won around to the idea. "Imagine getting through a geometry course in three weeks," one of them said to me. "It's preposterous! The children aren't making mistakes. How can they learn unless they make mistakes?"

That other fixed star of most programmers—immediate reinforcement—has also come in for a share of abuse. "Students who are highly anxious about their work perform better if they are not told how they are doing," says Dr. Ernest R. Hilgard of Stanford University.

Nevertheless, immediate reinforcement, errorless learning, and the freedom of every student to learn at his own speed must be adjudged the prime goals of the new psychology in education. Of the techniques which programmers use to achieve these goals we have already discussed three: the single unit of information per frame, the short mental distance between frames, and the use of questions and answers to string frames together. There are other tactics such as repetition, cueing, and the use of vanishing stimuli. Of these, repetition speaks for itself while the other two bear further explanation.

In elementary courses, the cue is a device to help the student make a correct response. It may simply by a parallel grammatical structure in the unit of information and the related question. It may also be the appearance of a key word in capital letters. Invariably this word turns out to be the answer to one of the questions.

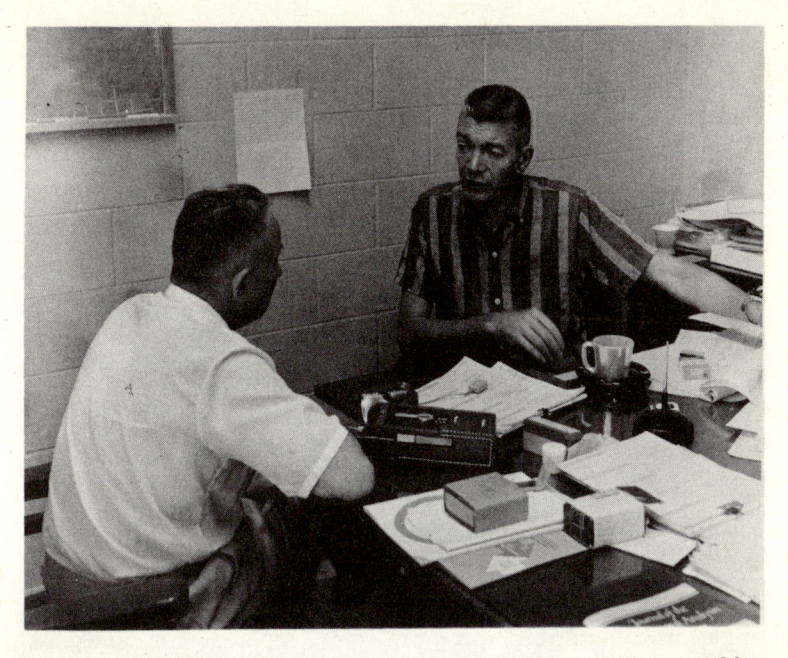

I am taping the record of my discussion of the teaching machine program with Dr. Lloyd Homme, president of Teaching Machines, Inc., Albuquerque.

The vanishing technique is extremely effective. Herbert Terrace used it on his pigeons at Harvard when he taught them to respond first to a red light, then to a red light with vertical stripes, and finally to vertical stripes without the color. In his article for *Scientific America*, Dr. Skinner described how the technique was applied to the teaching of geography:

"In teaching a map the machine asks the student to describe spatial relations among cities, countries, rivers and so on, as shown on a fully labeled map. He is then asked to do the same with a map in which the names have been partially

59

'vanished'—that is, removed in whole or in part. Eventually he is asked to report the same relations with no map at all. If the material has been well programmed, he should be able to do so with few, if any, errors."

Techniques of programming are moving toward greater complexity, greater refinement and higher ambitions all at the same time. Within a year or two we will look back on the programs of today as primitive. And, in time, we will develop superior programs.

"Not a day passes but that we don't learn something new about programming. Programs often seem obsolete and archaic the day after they are written," says David Padwa, president of Basic Systems.

Even though the initial cost now appears prohibitive, while the new programs and advanced teaching machines are being introduced, the total teaching costs will drop drastically. A single mimeographed program may replace thousands of textbooks.

Programmed material will be available not only for schools and colleges but for adults, industry, military services and underdeveloped nations. The machines and programs must be so developed that they are educationally sound. The research that the manufacturers are doing now will determine whether the teaching-machine movement will continue to grow and expand as dynamically and dramatically as it has within the last several years.

High academic standards must be maintained, or else criticism of the program will reflect on the technique.

1. This is a pile of pebbles.

   The pebbles are easy to see because they are large. If you make them smaller, you have sand. If you make them still _____, you have powder.

ANSWER TO QUESTION 1:

smaller

2. If you keep making powder particles smaller, you eventually end up with atoms. Why can't we see atoms?

   All matter is made up of atoms. Does this mean that you are made up of atoms?

   (yes/no)

ANSWER TO QUESTION 2:

They are too small.

yes

3. The center of the atom is called the nucleus. Label the nucleus of each atom.

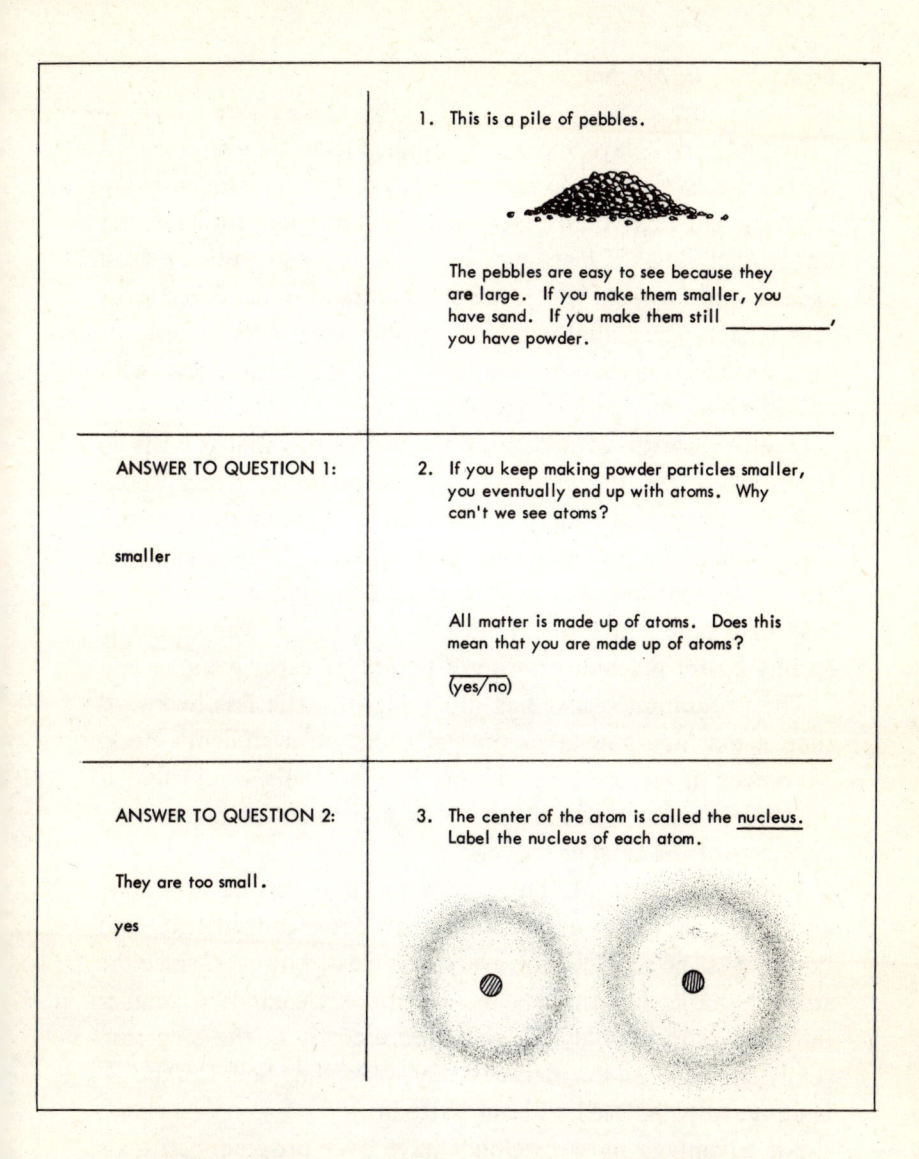

Sample page from a program issued by Basic Systems, Inc.

Books Versus Machines

In the "early" days, most programmed learning was prepared for the mechanical teaching machine. Today, there are far more programmed texts than machines, and although both use the same psychology of learning (with one major exception), both have won followings which are sometimes at odds. Since most researchers agree that students profit from either form of programmed instruction, the debate is concerned less with philosophies than with practicalities.

One obvious disadvantage of the machine is that it costs so much more than the programmed text or book. When Rockville Centre, Long Island, introduced a programmed algebra text, it did so on a strictly experimental basis. Quite logically it wanted to see how well programmed learning worked before making a major investment. Just as logically, it was unwilling to buy costly machines during a period of experiment.

The programmed text has other merits. It is less awkward than a machine and takes up less room on a student's desk. Moreover, it can be taken home. Few students would find it convenient to carry a machine back and forth for homework, even one of the smaller models.

Unlike the textbook, however, a machine can be used over and over again with only minor wear. Programmed texts and books must be replaced for every new class, however, since the student marks his answers in. The book demands a smaller initial investment, but it may be more costly in the long run. (Only one book on the market today—"Spelling Self-Taught"—is designed to be used without write-ins.)

An advantage most machines have over programmed texts is a built-in grading device. Machines keep a record of a student's right and wrong answers, and this record is available

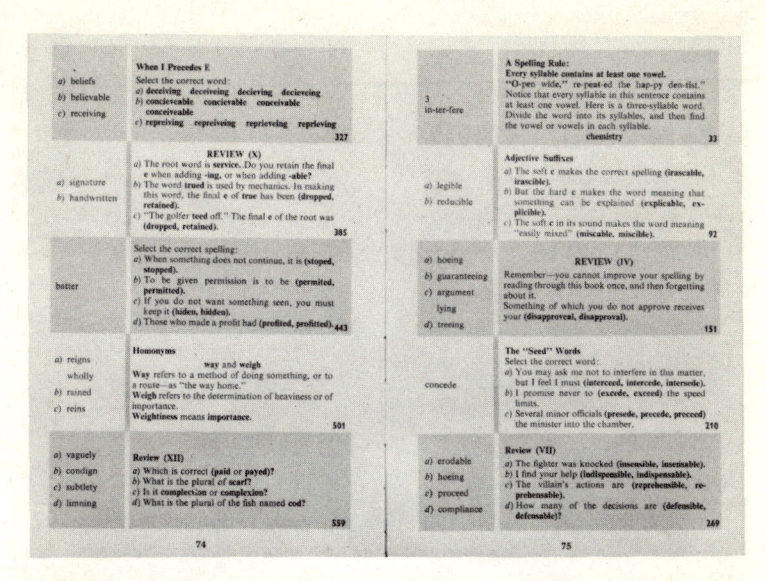

Sample page from the teaching-machine book, "Spelling Self-Taught," with multiple-choice type of frames.

to the teacher as soon as the course is finished. The amount of time she would have to spend grading a text would be exhausting.

Another possible disadvantage of programmed books is that students occasionally take shortcuts and peek at answers. While books have not yet been made cheat-proof, machines prevent the student from looking ahead before writing his answer and the answer, once it is written, cannot be erased or changed. The book makes cheating easy.

When I talked with some of the students at Rockville Centre, I found they were disconcerted by the fact that they had almost to close their eyes when they turned from page to page in a programmed text to avoid cheating.

"I try not to look," one student told me. Another said, "I

Students in Rockville Centre, N.Y., working on an E.B.F.-Temac program.

know it's wrong to look ahead, but sometimes when I'm in a hurry and I think the bell is going to ring to end the class, I glance ahead so I can finish the page I'm working on."

Still, in the face of this evidence, Dr. Homme told me he believes cheating will not be a problem. His main argument is that if a student is graded on the basis of weekly, monthly, or semester tests, he will gain nothing by cutting corners during periods of study.

Later I talked with a ninth grade boy who was using the kind of programmed book that has questions on the left and answers on the right, but with a mask covering the answers. Not until after he writes his answer is he supposed to pull the mask down a notch and check to see if he was right. To learn how Dr. Homme's theory turned out in practice, I asked the youngster if he ever cheated.

"What's the good of cheating?" he answered. "We don't get marked for our answers. It's the weekly quizzes that count. If I don't do the work now, I won't be able to pass the tests."

2331. A binomial factor of the sum of two cubes will be the _____ of the numbers that are cubed. To factor the sum of two cubes, first write the _____ factor.

sum, binomial

2332. The first term of the trinomial factor of the sum of two cubes will be the _____ of the _____ term of the binomial factor.

square, first

2333. The second term of the trinomial factor will be minus the _____ of the two terms of the _____ factor.

product, binomial

2334. The last term of the trinomial factor will be the _____ of the _____ term of the binomial factor.

square, last

2335. _____ is the binomial factor of x^3+8.

$x+2$

2336. $x+2$ is the binomial factor of x^3+8. The square of x is equal to _____; minus the product of x and 2 is _____; the square of 2 is _____.

x^2
$-2x$
4

2337. Complete the following factorization:
$x^3+8=(x+2)($ _____ $)$

x^2-2x+4

2338. _____ is the binomial factor of x^3+8y^3.

$x+2y$

Here is a page from the course this boy used. It is the E.B.F.-Temac algebra used experimentally in hundreds of high schools this year. On the right-hand side of the page is the masked flap. First you write the answer, then you pull the flap down question by question, compare your answer with the correct one, and continue.

Despite arguments about the vulnerability of programmed books to cheating, they are being introduced in hundreds of school systems every month. Although they lack the manipulative excitement and strangeness of machines, they are much more numerous. Machines have their greatest following today in the military services, in business training and in adult education. Perhaps the final word on the debate over programmed books and machines is that neither is fundamentally superior to the other. Both may give a revolutionary uplift to American education.

Programmed learning, however, is no longer solely an American product. It has left our shores and has gone abroad. It has been introduced in Italy, France, Greece, Germany, and the Federation of Rhodesia.

In the International Trade Fair held at Turin, Italy, in the fall of 1961, eighteen students from Valfre High School in Turin took a programmed plane geometry course in an Italian translation while thousands of Fair visitors watched. (This course, and one in algebra, also translated into Italian, are to be used on a trial basis by some 2,000 students in thirty schools throughout Italy.)

The Valfre students worked five days a week in a model classroom in the Fair's American Pavilion. Under the direction of Professor Rasalba Copelli, a teacher-consultant, they completed an average of sixty frames at each of two daily fifty-minute class sessions. This geometry course is broken down into 11,290 tiny frames, arranged in a logical sequence. The information is simple at first and gradually becomes more advanced. As in the other programmed learning courses, the student works at his own rate, under the teacher's supervision, responding to each frame before moving on to the next. He is tested at intervals by the teacher.

A high school math teacher introduces the first programmed learning course overseas. The scene is Valfre High School, Turin, Italy, and the students are taking a geometry course in a "school room" that is part of the American exhibit at the International Trade Fair.

Said Dr. Maurice B. Mitchell, president of Encyclopaedia Britannica Films, whose course was the one used: "We are pleased by the keen interest in programmed instructional materials overseas. Just as educators in the United States are finding that programmed materials relieve teachers of routine drill and allow them to enrich their curricula and spend more time with students who need attention, so educators in Italy and elsewhere abroad are beginning to appreciate that this new tool holds great promise for them, too."

The most significant controversy in programmed learning today is not over the merits of books and machines but over two kinds of books. More exactly, it deals with the different philosophies of programming these books represent.

In Chapter Two I talked about Joseph Blumenthal's "English 2600" and Crowder and Martin's "Adventures in Algebra."

The first book has a Skinner type of program; it asks questions that require a student to make original responses, and in some examples, make multiple choices. While the second book also uses questions and answers, its special technique is multiple-choice. When a student uses "Adventures in Algebra," he does not think up his own answers but selects them from lists of two or three alternatives.

Dr. Crowder and Dr. Skinner vigorously oppose each other's programs, and the nub of their debate is errorless learning.

"Multiple-choice questions are the greatest evil in American education," Skinner has said. "Effective multiple-choice material must contain plausible wrong answers, which are out of place in the delicate process of shaping behavior . . . Every wrong answer on a multiple-choice test increases the probability that a student will some day dredge out of his imperfect memory the wrong answer instead of the right one."

A Skinner text moves from question to question in a tight straight line, giving the student little chance to detour into side-alleys of error. A Crowder text is not so neat. Its multiple-choices send the student scrambling back and forth over the pages, seeking explanations for his correct and incorrect answers. If he says three times three is ten, he is directed to a page which tells him why he is wrong. Then he is directed back to the question and told to try again. On the other hand, a student who decides three times three equals nine is spared further lecturing on the subject and proceeds at once to the next stage of information. This "branching" technique, as it is known among programmers, allows the bright student to skip many portions of the text. The less gifted student gets more detailed instruction. In this way a Crowder book acts like a flexible, patient tutor.

129
[from page 125]

YOUR ANSWER: In ordinary arithmetic, it is not always true that, if a, b, and c are numbers, $a(b + c) = ab + ac$.

Well, let's get at it this way. Suppose you were selling magazine subscriptions. For every subscription you sold you earned 50 cents. On Monday you sold two subscriptions; on Wednesday you sold three subscriptions; on Saturday you sold one subscription.

Now, there are two ways of figuring up how much money you made. You can either (1) figure the amount of money you earned each day and then add these daily amounts to give you the total for the week, or (2) keep track of the number of subscriptions you sold each day and then figure your earnings at the end of the week by multiplying the total number of subscriptions sold by 50 cents.

(1) Monday: 2 subscriptions @ 50¢ = 2 × .50 = $1.00
    Wednesday: 3 subscriptions @ 50¢ = 3 × .50 = 1.50
    Saturday: 1 subscription @ 50¢ = 1 × .50 =   .50
                       Total weekly earnings: $3.00

(2) Monday: 2 subscriptions
    Wednesday: 3 subscriptions
    Saturday: 1 subscription
    Weekly total: 6 subscriptions

    Weekly earnings: 6 subscriptions @ 50¢ = 6 × .50 = $3.00

So you see, if two or more numbers are to be multiplied by the same number, they can be either multiplied individually and then added together or added together first and then multiplied; it makes no difference in the result.

Now return to page 125 and choose the correct answer.

125
[from page 128]

YOUR ANSWER: If $y = 3(5 + 4)$, $y = 27$.

You are correct. The 3 multiplies the entire quantity inside the parentheses. So if
$$y = 3(5 + 4),$$
$$y = 3(9) = 27.$$

Now, we would get the same result in this case if, instead of adding the two numbers inside the parentheses and then multiplying by 3, we first multiplied each number inside the parentheses by 3 and then added the products together.

$$y = 3(5 + 4)$$
$$y = 3(5) + 3(4)$$
$$y = 15 + 12 = 27$$

In ordinary arithmetic is it always true that, if a, b, and c are numbers,
$$a(b + c) = ab + ac?$$

Yes. **page 121**

No. **page 129**

This is the way an algebra course looks in the Crowder scrambled book, the Tutor Text called "Adventures in Algebra."

Dr. Crowder, who is almost a minority of one in the debate, believes the Skinner approach is too one-sided. "Problem-solving is a very intricate form of behavior," he says. "We should be under no temptation to reduce it merely to a series of rote associations. Furthermore, no two people have the same degree of intelligence. It is not necessary to send bright students willy-nilly through each step of a program designed to educate the dullest minds."

Who is right? Though my own views are close to Dr. Skinner's, I can see no quick resolution of the argument. Both kinds of programmed texts are being used to day, and with the passage of time they may turn out to be more complementary than antagonistic. In the meantime we can turn our attention to other questions.

How, for instance, do students respond?

CHAPTER FOUR

How Do Students Respond?

Education is the pursuit of excellence. But in this pursuit, children seldom realize what they are striving for. Abstractions like "excellence" are, after all, hard for young minds to grasp. Nevertheless, we *can* give children goals which make sense to them, which at a simple day-to-day level give them encouragement and a desire to learn.

There is nothing profound or academic about this kind of encouragement. In a teaching machine it is simply the repeated sense of achievement which comes from making correct answers. In a traditional classroom it is a good mark on a test, a pat on the back, a smile or a "well done" from the teacher.

This noon my daughter Carla ran into my room with a poem she had written a week earlier for her high school English class. On it the teacher had penciled, "Excellent treatment. Shows maturity and rare insight."

"This is fine, Carla," I said proudly. "How do you feel?"

"Oh, I feel terrific," she answered. "Daddy, you know I'll really have to work hard now. I just can't let my teacher down."

Unfortunately, such encouragement is a rare thing in the daily school life of the average child. This can be seen when you walk into any classroom with 20 or more children. A youngster thinks he knows the correct answer and raises his hand. The teacher calls on him; he is right. The next time he knows the answer he will again raise his hand. This time, however, he may not be called upon to respond. There are 19 other children in the class who must be given a chance. This forced neglect occurs again and again. Why call on Johnny? Johnny knows his answers. Call on someone who doesn't know. Thus we see how Johnny is held back by the average children in the class, who in turn move too quickly for the slowest children. Operating on all the youngsters, bright or dull, is the same rigid, negative homogeneity of "You better study, or else . . ."

I have talked with many children who were using teaching machines, and their remarks are the best endorsement of the healthy psychological climate of programmed learning. Many of their comments appear in the latter part of this chapter. Meanwhile, it is wise to bear in mind that a school's function is deeper than merely teaching facts and ideas. What it should strive for is the creation of an open, elastic intelligence in its children. Such receptivity is all but throttled by the aversive discipline of most present-day schools. When a child studies to avoid the consequences of not studying, he becomes a tactician, a little master of opportunity, learning only those things which will pacify the teacher or get him over the predictable terrain of the next exam. He loses whatever sense of wonder and excitement he may have had about knowledge.

Time Savings

There are many ways to gauge the different, saner environment of programmed learning. One of these is measuring the reduction in study time.

Evidence gathered from experiments at Roanoke, Albuquerque, Rockville Centre, and elsewhere suggest that the time needed to master any given course can be cut from 30 to 50 per cent by programmed instruction!

This is true both on the school and college level.

At Collegiate School for Boys in New York City: students finished a mathematics course in half the time it took a control group to do it. Freshmen at Hamilton College went through a program of logic in one-third less time than normal.

At Ohio University: students finished a course in 20 per cent less time after it was programmed as a Crowder "scrambled" book.

At Bellevue Public Schools, Washington: seventh-grade youngsters taking an algebra course usually given to eighth- or ninth-graders finished a semester (four months) of study in two months.

At Columbia University: a student wrote a perfect exam paper after completing one term of math in a little over four hours!

In addition to saving time, teaching machines generally encourage students to do better work. When my daughter Carla was in tenth grade last Fall, she had trouble with geometry. It was her roughest subject, and small wonder. Within a matter of weeks she had three different teachers. The first teacher left and was replaced by a substitute. The substitute was drafted into the Army and a third teacher just out of college took over. He was nervous. So was my daughter.

Plane Geometry

2878. On the quadrilateral $ABCD$ we are given a pair of sides equal. We are given that _____ and _____ are equal.

AD, BC

2879. We are also given that AD and BC are _____.

parallel

2880. We are required to prove that $CD =$ _____.

AB

2881. On the figure of figure 246 let us mark AD and CB each with a double mark to remind us that they are _____.

equal

2882. We shall give a formal proof of this proposition but let us first see why it is true. So far we have only two methods of showing that a pair of lines are equal. One method is to show that the pair of lines are _____ _____ _____ of congruent triangles.

corresponding sides (or corresponding parts)

2883. We would also know that a pair of lines are equal if they are two sides of a triangle which are _____ two angles of a triangle which we already know to be equal.

opposite

2884. On figure 246, AB and CD cannot be two sides of a triangle which are opposite equal angles. Our best hope would be to prove that AB and CD are corresponding parts of _____ triangles.

congruent

2885. One method of getting two triangles which we may be able to prove are congruent is to draw the line _____.

AC (DB would be just as good)

2886. On figure 246 we may draw either the line AC or the line DB. To be definite let us draw the line AC. We want to show that $\triangle DAC$ and _____ are congruent.

$\triangle BCA$

2887. We remember that when we write $\triangle DAC \cong \triangle BCA$ we mean that the two triangles can be made to coincide with
    point D corresponding to point B,
    point A corresponding to point _____,
    point C corresponding to point _____.

C
A

2888. We already know that $DA =$ _____.

BC

Sample TEMAC page.

Earlier I had received an Encyclopaedia Britannica Films program in tenth-grade geometry. "Carla, why don't you try this?" I said. "It might help." Reluctantly, she agreed, despite a parting rejoinder that she was sure she wouldn't like it.

Two hours later she came downstairs. "I was wrong, Daddy," she said. "This makes sense." Carla had finished the program's first 200 frames. When I gave her the E.B.F. test, she answered 90 per cent of the questions correctly. A week later she finished frames 200 to 600. Once again she breezed through the test with a high grade. Carla never did read the entire E.B.F. programmed book, but she learned enough to make geometry interesting. The upshot? She began to get grades of 95, and geometry became her favorite subject.

This is not an isolated example. I have seen many students at work in various courses, and programmed learning seems to have a salutary effect on the great majority of them. At Williams College in 1871, James A. Garfield said, "A pine bench with Mark Hopkins at the edge and me at the foot is a good enough college for me." A growing number of psychologists believe that the teaching machine is every student's personal Mark Hopkins.

When a youngster fails a course, his failure is not only a reflection on himself but an indictment of the system that was supposed to teach him. It is for this reason that programmed learning may prove to be the greatest educational discovery of our generation. A teaching machine very seldom fails a child. He may go slowly or brilliantly fast, but when he comes to the end of a program he must understand what he has read. The question-answer technique prevents him from glossing over material that, in any ordinary textbook, would remain incomprehensible to him.

Thus, when eighth-graders at Manhasset Junior High School (New York) finished "English 2600" in $12\frac{1}{2}$ hours, they were

183.

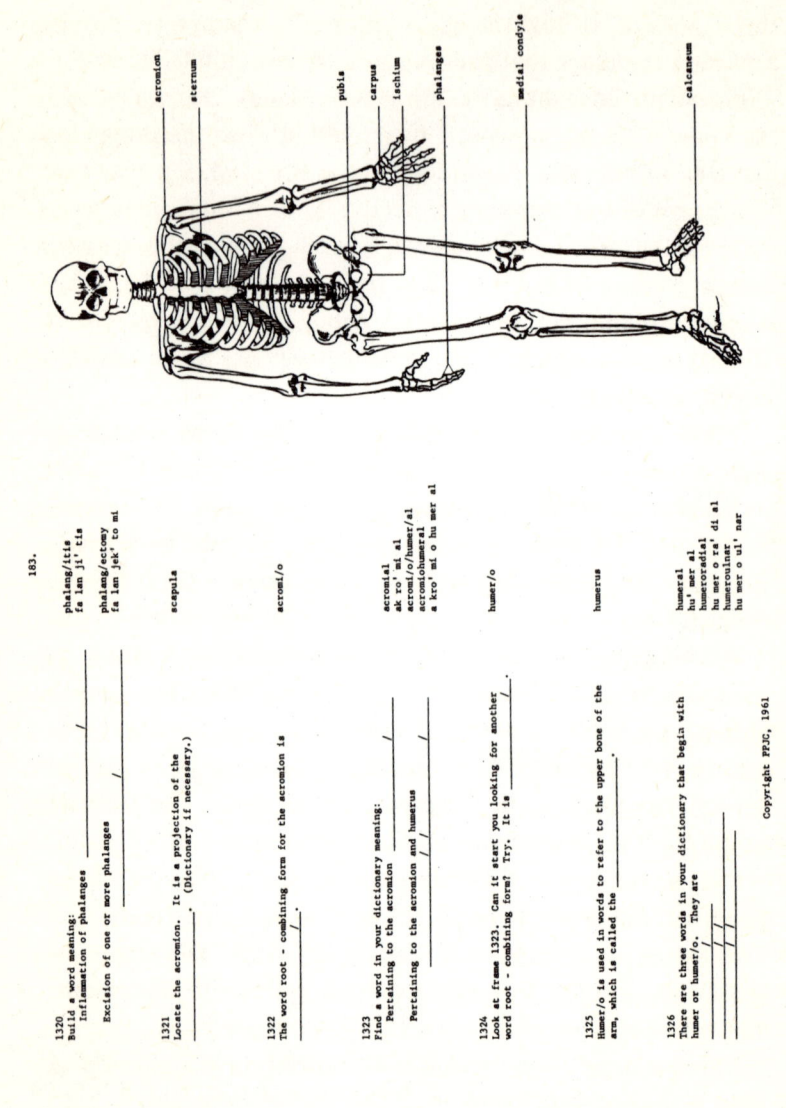

```
                                                         acromion
                                                         sternum


                                                         pubis
                                                         carpus
                                                         ischium
                                                         phalanges

                                                         medial condyle


                                                         calcaneum
```

1320
Build a word meaning:
  Inflammation of phalanges _____   phalang/itis
                                                            fa lan ji' tis

  Excision of one or more phalanges _____   phalang/ectomy
                                                          fa lan jek' to mi

1321
Locate the acromion. It is a projection of the
_____. (Dictionary if necessary.)   scapula

1322
The word root - combining form for the acromion is
_____.   acromi/o

1323
Find a word in your dictionary meaning:
  Pertaining to the acromion _____   acromial
                                     ak ro' mi al
  Pertaining to the acromion and humerus _____   acromi/o/humer/al
                                         acromiohumeral
                                         a kro' mi o hu mer al

1324
Look at frame 1323. Can it start you looking for another
word root - combining form? Try. It is
_____.   humer/o

1325
Humer/o is used in words to refer to the upper bone of the
arm, which is called the _____   humerus

1326
There are three words in your dictionary that begin with
humer or humer/o. They are
_____   humeral
_____   hu' mer al
_____   humeroradial
           hu mer o ra' di al
           humeroulnar
           hu mer o ul' nar

Copyright PPJC, 1961

These are some samples of the Point Park medical technology course.

learning a year's worth of grammar with a comprehension no ordinary textbook could match. Nor could normal methods of instruction have had the same effect as programmed learning on the medical technology class at Pittsburgh's Point Park Junior College where a failure rate dropped from 12 per cent to 3 per cent, while the course time was cut from 120 to 30 hours!

Does this suggest that the teacher is not necessary? Dr. Bell, the instructor at Point Park, answered that question for me. "Of course I'm needed," he said. "I find that I can give my students better instruction. They learn the basic facts of medical technology at home, with their programmed book. In class we discuss many issues relating to the course that I was unable to touch upon in the past.

"Will a machine ever replace me? If I can't do a better job than a machine then I deserve to be replaced!"

Even 4- and 5-year olds can be taught to use the teaching machine as I found out when I watched youngsters in Albuquerque. The laboratories there have developed a machine (the Min-Max) that is simple for a child to use.

For example, the child sees what is obviously a rabbit. He then sees three words—ring, rabbit and cat. He is instructed to encircle the word that matches the picture. He encircles rabbit, and then he finds out that he is right. So he goes to the next frame. This presupposes that he can recognize the letters in rabbit, and connect the word with the picture.

"We are getting the children ready to read," explained Dr. L. Benjamin Wyckoff, inventor of the machine, and chairman of TMI board of directors. "By the time a child finishes a complete set of these reading frames, he should understand many words, and be ready to start the actual process of classroom reading."

"This is fun," said a young 5-year-old as she guessed the right word time and again.

"I want to go to school so I can learn to read more," added another, a 4½-year-old cherub of a girl.

"When I get a wrong word I ask my teacher and she tells me which is the right one," another young lass volunteered.

Why can't Johnny read? Because he never took the Wyckoff teaching-machine program!

Some Sample Programs

> 1) **Manufacture** means to make or build. *Chair factories manufacture chairs.* Copy the word here:
> ☐ ☐ ☐ ☐ ☐ ☐ ☐ ☐ ☐ ☐
> 2) Part of the word is like part of the word **factory.** Both parts come from an old word meaning to *make* or *build.*
> **manu** ☐ ☐ ☐ ☐ **ure**
> 3) Part of the word is like part of the word **manual.** Both parts come from an old word for *hand.* Many things used to be made by hand.
> ☐ ☐ ☐ ☐ **facture**
> 4) The same letter goes in both spaces:
> **m** ☐ **nuf** ☐ **cture**
> 5) The same letter goes in both spaces:
> **man** ☐ **fact** ☐ **re**
> 6) Chair factories
> ☐ ☐ ☐ ☐ ☐ ☐ ☐ ☐ ☐ ☐
> chairs.

Here is a sample of how a third-grade child learns to spell, as proposed by Dr. Skinner. The child, you will notice, learns (presumably) to spell the word MANUFACTURE in six frames.

This same principle is followed in other subjects. Give the child a small bit of information at a time. Make sure that he masters it. Then go on to the next step. Be sure that he makes few errors. Give him plenty of encouragement. Baby him if necessary. Make him feel as though learning is a pleasure, not a chore. Don't threaten or punish.

A TEACHING-MACHINE SAMPLER
(High School Physics)

Frame	Answer
1. The important parts of a flashlight are the battery and the bulb. When we "turn on" a flashlight, we close a switch which connects the battery with the _____.	bulb
2. When we turn on a flashlight, an electric current flows through the fine wire in the _____ and causes it to grow hot.	bulb
3. When the hot wire glows brightly, we say that it gives off or sends out heat and _____.	light
4. The fine wire in the bulb is called a filament. The bulb "lights up" when the filament is heated by the passage of a(n) _____ current.	electric
5. When a weak battery produces little current, the fine wire, or _____, does not get very hot.	filament
6. A filament which is *less* hot sends out or gives off _____ light.	less

---

Here, for example, is a sample frame from a high school physics course. How can you go wrong?

The Bright Student

Time-saving is important. We should note, however, that most cases quoted deal with students in the mass, and that educators have grown increasingly concerned with students at more distinct levels of ability. What impact does programmed learning have on the exceptionally gifted child?

You may find as much difference in ability as seven years in a conventional fourth-grade class. Some children may read at first-grade level, and others at eighth-grade. The teacher, with 35 children, can give only one or two minutes to each one. The bright child gets almost nothing, the average child a bit more, while the slow child gets the bulk of the limited time.

It's probably accurate to say that the bright student is not getting the education he deserves. James B. Conant, president-emeritus of Harvard University, estimates that the vast majority of students who rank high in academic ability are receiving insufficient attention.

It is shocking that so large a number of our brighter boys and girls never complete high school or college. We are wasting a tremendous amount of our human resources. Three out of ten of our bright high school graduates do not graduate from college. Only half of those who enter college remain to graduate. Something has gone wrong.

The teaching machine has great value for the gifted student, simply because it lets him learn as fast and as well as he can. We have seen that this does not happen in the normal classroom. Halfway through a course, the bright student begins to get bored. He may have read several chapters ahead in his textbook and understood them all, but the teacher has adjusted her pace to the rest of the class. She cannot give him the special encouragement, assignments, and tests he needs if he is to remain alert. Consequently he begins day-dreaming and staring out the window. He may even fall behind because he is so far ahead.

Many studies and my own observations suggest that the talented student accomplishes much more with programmed learning than with ordinary methods. So much more, in fact that some teachers have disapproved of machines because they make learning easy. They seem to think that education should require intense effort and perspiration, as if it were a form of calisthenics. That the exact opposite is the case I think has been demonstrated by Dr. Skinner in his experiments with reinforcement and errorless learning.

Actually, programmed learning must be judged not by its superficial easiness but by its results. So far the results have been good. There is no longer any doubt that it reduces the time needed for study, or that it lowers the frequency of failures. We also know that it can break the bottleneck in our educational system which so often regiments, frustrates, and ultimately defeats our brightest students.

I think most teachers are aware of this. They want to treat each student as an individual, but the system is as unresponsive to them as it is to the students. Whenever they get the chance to help a bright student, they leap at it.

I spoke with one of Larry Hill's teachers in Roanoke shortly after he had been put through an experimental program in mathematics. "Larry kept me on my toes," she said. "No sooner did he finish geometry than I got him started on trigonometry. He romped through that, and then he finished up with calculus. By that time he knew as much as I did. If the semester hadn't ended, I would have been in trouble."

In Albuquerque I talked to a 13-year-old girl who had finished a programmed algebra course. She was a bright ninth-grade student and had spent only three weeks on the course. Her final mark was 95.

"Didn't you have trouble finishing a six-month course in three weeks?" I asked.

"Why no," she said. "It was easy."

"Does she really know algebra?" I asked her instructor.

"She certainly does, at least judging by conventional tests," he said.

We watch a 13-year-old taking an algebra test with a Min-Max teaching machine.

The achievements of Larry Hill and the youngster in Albuquerque are the best arguments for teaching bright students through programmed instruction. Could Larry have finished three math courses in one semester in the traditional classroom? Could the 13-year-old girl have learned algebra in three weeks? Probably not. The strength of teaching machines in this area is undeniable.

Thus far, no study has been made that compares teaching machines with honors classes, individual or seminar instruction, or rapid advance classes. However, several of the companies that prepare programmed instruction are doing research designed to make a comparison of the use of the teaching machine on the one hand, and the same material used in the enriched program of instruction. The question still remains: Will a student who takes a course in algebra in programmed instruction, for example, do as well or better if he takes that same course in a special enriched class environment?

We know that bright students do much better work when they take a course with a machine or programmed instruction. At the Syosset (N.Y.) public school, the principal divided his bright students into two groups with a medium of 126 I.Q. each (a superior I.Q. rating). One group was given Temac programmed instruction in algebra. Thirty-eight per cent of the Temac students were above the 90th percentile at the end of the course, compared with 21 per cent in the group using traditional methods. This difference is statistically significant.

Theoretically, the use of honors classes, individual instruction, small classes, better trained teachers, newer curricula materials and up-to-date textbooks should cut the gap between any teaching-machine group and a traditional class. But the point is that few schools employ these modern devices.

The Average Student

What about the average student? At Roanoke, it was found that 31 per cent of the eighth-graders who took a programmed course in algebra surpassed the national average of ninth-graders in the same subject. These students liked programmed learning; only 16 per cent of them favored a return to conventional methods. Elsewhere, I have observed that 85 to 90 per cent of the students prefer teaching machines.

In experiments with average students at Rockville Centre, Long Beach (New York), Palo Alto, and elsewhere, programmed learning has almost always resulted in better grades.

An elementary school class in Huntington, N.Y., is divided, with half of the students using Min-Max teaching machines and the other half using conventional books.

Differences between bright and average students are translated more into speed than into test scores, although grade distinctions still do exist. The A student who normally took a year to complete a course may now finish it in five months, two months, or three weeks, while maintaining his A grade. The average student who formerly received a C for a year's work may now finish it in seven months while getting a B plus or A minus. Thus, the average student will improve, but a teaching machine will never make him over into a genius. What it does is remove the sense of inferiority that dogs him when his grades are considerably lower than those of gifted students. When you test an average student on a programmed course, his scores may come quite close to those of a brighter student. The main difference is that he will be on frame 550 when the bright student is on frame 1000.

The Below-Average Student

Does the below-average child gain and retain what he learns? In a study made by Professor Douglas Porter of Harvard University to see how effective the teaching machine was in teaching spelling to elementary school children, he found that students did improve in their knowledge of spelling as compared with children using the traditional method. But even more significant was the by-product he found: the greatest gains in spelling were made by students in the lowest I.Q. category. Programmed learning gave them a form of encouragement they had never experienced before.

The Retarded Student

All the qualities of programmed learning which operate on bright or average students also work an advantage for the student who is physically or mentally retarded or emotionally disturbed. In the first place, he, too, is allowed to go along at his own rate. He is not abused because he is unable to keep up with a "class." Since he is not asked to compete in open class exercises, he seldom experiences the horror of being called a dunce by his schoolmates.

The emotionally disturbed child soon learns that the teaching machine does not lose its patience, does not become sarcastic, does not upbraid him because of his personal problems. You might say a good teacher does not do this either—and I would agree. Unfortunately, we still have many teachers who, because they're overworked, underpaid, and saddled with extra-curricular duties, are unable to maintain the equilibrium that is especially important for the disturbed child. As a result, he drops further and further behind and grows more disheartened every day.

Such, of course, is not the case with a teaching machine. Slow or emotionally disturbed students like the machine because it constantly engages them. They are active, not passive, agents in the educational process. They are given a real chance to do something, prove themselves. It is as though each child had a teacher of his own.

I spoke to a girl who was starting her second year in a programmed course on geometry. She wasn't particularly dull but she was very slow. Her parents' divorce had left her feeling adrift and helpless.

"Aren't you a little bored, doing this for the second year?" I asked.

"Oh, no," she said with enthusiasm. "Not at all. I'm beginning to understand now, and I like it."

A young boy said to me, "I never liked algebra until I got this machine. Now I know what I'm doing."

He's a better student now, even though it took him three semesters to finish a one-semester course. At least he's no longer disheartened and is trying hard to learn. In the traditional program, he would have received an F at the end of the first semester and probably after the second and third semesters, too. Now he's proving he can learn.

It well may be that the emotionally disturbed or retarded child is not really dull. He may simply need more time for his work. I don't think speed is the equivalent of intelligence, although most classrooms operate as if it were. At the end of a period the teacher calls out, "That's all! Examination is over. Put your pencils away and let me have your papers." There's a muffled protest from a handful of students whose complaints run something like, "Oh, if only I had another half-hour. I could have finished the test and passed it for sure." When they get their scores of 40 or 50 they think, "That's that. This course is too tough for me."

Why shouldn't these children have another half-hour? What is the logic behind forcing all students, regardless of their speed, to work at the same rate? If one child can read a chapter in 10 minutes and another takes one hour, all we can say is that the first student is much faster. Whether or not he's more brilliant is still open to question. Perhaps this irrational demand for quickness is the reason why Einstein did poorly in elementary mathematics and Winston Churchill muddled through English. When both men had time to think, they did superb work.

The end result of working at different speeds is that some may finish college at 12 or 14, others at 22 or 25. But no student will be humiliated, embarrassed or belittled in the process. Tensions are bound to decrease and nervous maladies (even student suicides) decline when we substitute rewards for scorn.

In my opinion, the best thing about teaching machines is the way they allow every student to work at his own speed and fullest capacity. In Albuquerque, a teacher gave me an example of the tremendous encouragement this gives disturbed or retarded youngsters. "You see little Johnny there?" he said. "He's been with me now for three weeks. When he came here his parents were despondent. He couldn't speak a word. He's either emotionally disturbed or mentally retarded. I don't know which yet. Now, after three weeks of programmed learning, he's beginning to recognize words. I dare say that within another several weeks, he'll be able to recognize words and actually read."

Another teacher at Albuquerque said to me, "This morning I worked with a child of 9. Four weeks ago when his mother brought him in, we gave him a pre-test and he didn't know a single word. Now he's able to sound out approximately 50 words and recognize them."

His mother was amazed at his progress. "Why, I just can't believe it," she told the instructor. "What did you do to him?"

"I just let him go at his own rate," he answered. "I encouraged him and was sympathetic. It's mostly a matter of confidence. These children have lost confidence because they can't read like the other kids. When they aren't helped, their behavior eventually turns anti-social. I don't let this happen. I encourage them. The machines encourage them, too."

One child I saw had come to the laboratory a week previously, unable to read a word. He was working on a Min-Max and was learning to read, write, and spell a dozen new words a day. At the end of his hour-long session with the machine, he picked it up and showed it to me. "This is mine," he said. "It doesn't fuss at me. It doesn't yell. And I'm learning."

From the expression in his eyes, I guessed that he had been pushed around all his young life and felt he was finally doing something worthwhile.

Another child told me very gravely, "Everybody thought I was dumb. Now I'm showing them."

This pattern of new confidence and hope may not extend to every retarded or disturbed child, but it is pretty widespread. All students need reassurance; those who are retarded need it intensely. It was found that deaf children, who require a good deal of individual instruction and small classes, did better with machines than with teachers.

The Test Threat

I believe the American school system is one of the finest in the world, but it has its faults. Dr. Skinner has identified the principal villain in the whole piece: an antiquated philosophy of learning which is based on threats. Many teachers do not teach—they just assign and test. Ever since John Dewey introduced progressive education at the turn of the century, the birch-rod and dunce-cap psychology has been on the wane. In disguise, however, it survives in a deeply entrenched system of testing which, although not itself harmful, is often misused. I have heard teachers give several varieties of this little speech: "You kids have been noisy today. Okay, wait until you see the test I'm going to give you tomorrow. That'll teach you!"

Threats of this kind do not help educate any child, whether bright, retarded, or average. Could we teach a pigeon to play table tennis by threatening it? No, says Professor Skinner. Nor can we teach a child through threats. Teachers have asked me how they can maintain discipline without punishment. The answer, to my mind, is quite evident. Programmed learning imposes its own discipline. Children respond to the impartiality of the machine. It keeps their minds on their work, not because of threats or punishment, but because the work itself is enjoyable. Children respect the impartiality of the teaching machine. They like the reinforcement they get, and the privilege of learning at their own natural pace. In this new kind of school environment, there is no need for the old harsh discipline.

One of the key words in teaching-machine philosophy is "reinforcement." Studies by Professors Skinner, Homme, Holland and others have found that if you tell the pupil he has given the right answer, he will do better work. Ordinarily the student has to wait a day, a week or a month before he knows whether he made a good grade on his last test, or whether he got the algebra examples right. When he is "rewarded" with the right answer at once, he can puff out his chest, get a feeling of satisfaction, and continue to the next question with greater confidence.

At least, that is what the psychologists say, and that is the way it is evidently working out in practice.

"We think it is important that the student get immediate reinforcement," says Dr. David G. Salten, superintendent of schools in Long Beach (N.Y.), and one of the pioneers in the use of teaching machines. "The student wants to know whether he is right or wrong. This gives him the confidence that he needs as well as the incentive to continue. We now have a stronger, more effective teaching device. Let's make full use of it."

Do I hear a murmur of dissent? Of course. Some educators do not accept these conclusions.

Are we certain that, like the pigeon, the child wants to be rewarded or reinforced? Professor Ernest R. Hilgard of Stanford University isn't too certain. He comments: "With some kinds of tasks, high anxious learners perform better if not reminded how well (or how poorly) they are doing, while low anxious learners do better if they are interrupted with comments on their progress."

"Let's not make it too easy for the kids to learn," some educators keep saying. "If you give them everything on a silver platter, they'll expect to be babied all their lives. It's not easy to get an education. Make it tough on them."

Right here, on the record, I'll take a negative stand. I disagree. I think we can make learning easy, make it fun, connect it with real life, as John Dewey so passionately insisted.

It was easy for me to learn the word "spasebo," to learn how to pronounce it, and that it means "thanks." It was easy for

Carla to grasp the geometry fundamentals in one afternoon. It is easy for the child to spell the difficult word "manufacture" if led by the hand each step. It is easy to learn parts of the English language, and about the behavior of Pavlovian dogs.

Why should learning be boresome, distasteful, difficult?

Why make it unpleasant? Why insist on punishment, threats, shouts? We no longer use the whip, the cane, the cat-o'-nine-tails, the birch rod, the paddle, or the dunce stool very often. It is out of style.

We are slightly more subtle in our punishments to get the child to learn, to get him to behave, to instill discipline in him, to keep him in line. Twist the boy's arm; pull the girl's ear; box the lad's face; smack him over the head with a ruler. Anything to make him shut up, sit up and learn.

I have seen this aversive approach by even good teachers. I have shuddered with the same uneasiness that passes through me when I see a worried, nervous mother push spoonful after spoonful of distasteful cereal down her child's throat with the attendant screams of "EAT, EAT, DAMN YOU, EAT. IT'S GOOD FOR YOU."

"Will the use of rewards inhibit the child's ability to think for himself?" I asked Dr. Skinner.

"Not at all," he answered quickly and emphatically. "Just the contrary. By reinforcing the child, by encouraging him, by using rewards rather than punishment, we can get far more out of our children."

Then he added what we mentioned before: "A school system is a failure if it has to use threats to get children to learn. Aversive practices now in use must be replaced by more effective constructive techniques. Our entire system of teaching is based on wrong principles. You are not going to improve the education of a child by punishing him."

Teaching machines do not punish.

But, as Dr. Skinner points out, we now have a new method to teach children and adults, literate and illiterate, bright and dull, average and genius. We have a method to place a greater interaction between the teacher and the student.

We have entered the technological age. Few horses or mules remain in the military forces. We have seen the kitchen mechanized with refrigerators, dishwashers, automatic garbage disposal plants, electric dryers, electric can openers, and the deep freeze. The I.B.M. computer has been installed in business corporations. The automatic man can do everything but think—and now he is able to do that. Automation has replaced millions of unskilled laborers, and forced them to learn skills.

Every aspect of American life has been mechanized—except education. Why should the classroom be behind the times? Now, through teaching machines, education can join the 20th century. As Professor Skinner puts it: "The necessary techniques are known. The equipment needed can easily be produced. Nothing stands in the way but cultural inertia."

We stand on the threshhold of an educational and cultural renaissance. This renaissance will sweep old, horse-and-buggy teaching techniques into the footnotes of history. We have the skills, the brains, the know-how to meet the challenge of the Space Age. We have the imagination. The Electronic Age has entered the classroom, whether we will it or not.

In my opinion, if teaching machines do nothing more than call attention to the new psychology of learning, they will win their objective: a high standard of excellence in the American classroom.

How the Students Feel

Children know a good teacher from a poor one. They know a patient teacher from an impatient one. They know a kind teacher from a sarcastic one. They know the difference between a humane teacher and a heartless one. "Give us a good teacher, a teacher that doesn't yell, doesn't shout, doesn't play favorites, doesn't ignore us, doesn't treat us like dirt. That's all we want."

Time after time I heard youngsters say: "This teaching machine is patient, isn't it?" This doesn't speak well, of course, for their teachers. But it does speak well for the teaching machines.

"I flunked algebra last term," I was told by a student who had been taught in the traditional way. "On our first day in class the teacher said, 'Now take x and y and let's proceed from there.' That's exactly where she lost me. For the rest of the year I forgot about x and y and stared out of the window. In nine months I found how they build an apartment house from foundation to roof."

Programmed learning has its dissidents, too. "I don't like this work," a student said. "Machines bore me."

Fourteen-year-old Ellen was finishing her third week in an experimental algebra course when I stopped by to question her. Though an eighth-grader, she was taking a ninth-grade course.

"Have you ever taken algebra before?" I asked her.

"No, I haven't," she answered.

"What grade are you getting in the course?"

"I don't know. At the end of three weeks I understand what is being taught, but I haven't been tested. You see, I teach myself."

"How much time do you put in for study?"

"I take about 4 hours a week," she answered.

"So in about 96 hours you'll get a year's worth of algebra?" I asked.

"Well, that's what I've been told."

"Do you like the teaching machine, Ellen?"

"Yes, I really do. It's much better than when I had a teacher. I go as fast as I want and I don't have to worry about keeping up with somebody else."

"But doesn't it get boring to be alone?"

"Not for me," she answered. "It's not boring at all. I like it."

"What happens when you get stuck?" I asked. "If you can't get an answer, what do you do? I don't see any teachers around here."

"No, we don't have teachers, but we do have observers. If I can't answer a question I raise my hand and an observer comes and tells me what I'm doing wrong."

"How often do you call him?"

"Well, not really too often. You find out your mistakes right away, so you can correct them yourself."

"Do you think it's a good thing to know immediately whether you're right?"

"Why, of course! Everybody wants to know whether he's done right or wrong. When I get the right answer, it makes me feel good."

Next to Ellen was a girl named Joan. "What grade are you in, Joan?" I asked.

"I just finished high school," she said. "I'm 18."

The boy next to her was Harold Greenberg, a 16-year-old high school junior.

"What are you two working on?" I asked.

"Electricity," Harold said. "We don't know what level it's supposed to be. It's a course for the Navy and we're testing it before it gets approved. I guess it's about college level."

"How long have you been working on it?"

"This is our sixth week."

"Is it difficult?"

"Not at all," Joan answered. "We just take one step at a time."

"Do you like the machine?"

"Yes, I sure do."

"It's okay," Harold broke in.

"What's the best thing about it?" I asked.

"Being able to work at my own speed," Joan answered. Harold said: "Learning the program thoroughly. You can't get through it unless you do."

"What don't you like about it?"

"Not being able to go back and review what you've done. You can't reverse the machine. I guess we're supposed to remember everything we've read."

"How far do you think you'd be if this was a regular course in electricity, one that wasn't programmed for a machine?"

"I really don't know," Harold answered. "This is supposed to be a course that ordinarily takes a full year and we're more than halfway through after six weeks. Of course we can go a lot faster this way. In most schools the teacher has at least 25 kids and can't give you any attention. But we don't have to worry about anyone else here."

"How do you compare what you're doing with the machine and the way you'd be learning in a classroom?" I asked.

"I was pretty good in history," Harold said. "I can remember when I was way ahead and found it boring because I had read about it months before. In English everyone was ahead of me. I wondered, 'What's the good of going to class when I can never keep up?'"

"What about you, Joan?"

"Well, I guess I'm the opposite. I was ahead in English but behind in history. And I was way back in math."

"What did your teacher do?"

"For a whole semester I went to school early and stayed late so I could review math with her. Still, I barely scraped by with a C."

"And in this course in electricity?"

"Well, I think my average is about 90. The math part of it is easy. At school I was always nervous before an exam because I knew I wouldn't have time to finish it. Here you more or less test yourself at every step, so there's no time limit to worry about. Sometimes I did so poorly in math that the other kids laughed at me. I'm not overly sensitive, but I don't think it helped me. Nothing like that happens here. The other day we took our first test. Harold finished in 25 minutes and it took me 2 hours. So what? Nobody sat over us and told us to hurry."

"That's right," Harold said. "Another good point is that we got our scores as soon as we finished. We didn't have to wait a couple of weeks to find out whether we passed or not."

"Do you think this machine is as good as a real live teacher?" I asked.

"It's better than some of the teachers I've had," Harold said. When he saw my incredulous look he added, "Maybe you haven't seen some of the teachers I've had. Of course, there are some subjects where I'd want a teacher."

"What ones?"

"Well, mostly social studies, where there's a lot of discussion. I like a course where you can talk about what's going on, with the teacher."

"I do, too," Joan said. "In psychology I don't see how you could learn from a machine without a teacher. Still, I think I would have been better off last year if I'd had a machine in my

I am taping my interviews with students who have taken programmed instruction in statistics in Roanoke, Virginia.

senior-year sociology course. We used a textbook that was on the sixth-grade level. The teacher knew it was on the sixth-grade level but she said something about a budget and not being able to get new books. I told her the course was pretty boring. I know I could have gone much faster if I'd been allowed to."

"All I can say is that I like this machine but I certainly feel you can't replace a teacher," Harold said. "I would rather have both, half a period with the teacher and half with the machine."

"Yes, that sounds about right," Joan said. "Another thing—you can't cheat with the machine."

"Does much of that go on in the normal classroom?" I asked.

"Are you kidding?" she answered. "Everybody who has trouble passing is tempted to cheat, and at one time or another I think almost everybody has. You can't do that with a machine, though, because the machine only moves in one direction. You can't turn it back to change an answer."

"In a nutshell, then, you're both in favor of teaching machines?"

"Yes," Joan replied, "I think we learn more with them."

"I'll have to vote for the machine because it lets us take our time and go at our own pace," Harold answered. "Even so, I wouldn't want machines to be used in place of teachers for all our courses."

Richard G., a sophomore at the University of New Mexico, was taking a course in calculus at Albuquerque. When I spoke with him he had been using the machine for two weeks.

"How do you like it?" I asked.

"I'm getting along very nicely," he said. "I guess I would be up to about my second month of college work."

"Can you handle the subject without a human teacher?"

"Oh, yes. As you know the program is made up of small frames. You never get more than you can digest at one time. When I flunked calculus at the University last year, it was partly because the instructor handed out assignments in huge doses. He'd say, 'Read pages 20 to 65,' and I'd get lost somewhere around page 30. Of course, he had to do it that way. It was the nature of the class, and he just didn't have time to straighten out all my misconceptions. With the machine, every step is easy. I don't see how I can miss."

"I can spell infinitesimal, embarrassed, succumbed and other hard words," said a fourth-grader. "Spelling isn't hard when you use a machine."

A bright lad, I.Q. 170 plus, in a traditional program said to me: "I get bored in school. I finished my arithmetic book the first week, but our teacher said she had to use it for the rest of the year with the other children. Why can't I take more courses if I want to?" Why shouldn't he?

Another student was apprehensive about the simplicity of programmed learning. "I'm just amazed," he said. "In fact, I wasn't sure that I was getting it. I asked my instructor, 'Am I really learning statistics?' It seems so easy. I just hope I remember what I've gotten out of it."

A number of students expressed the same doubts. Work they once thought difficult now appeared simple to them, and they weren't sure they were really learning. Tests showed they were. The subjects hadn't been watered down; they covered as much ground just as thoroughly as before. What had been made easier was the learning process itself. The question-and-answer framing technique was new to the students, and they felt a little guilty about it because, like most of us, they had been led to believe that learning is a difficult, onerous process. This attitude should disappear as programmed learning becomes commonplace in our schools.

How long *will* the information stay with them? No one knows. How much stays with any of us? Tests show that factual information disappears fast.

Psychologists feel that students get the same amount of retention with the machine that they would without. One of them put it this way:

"The maximization of achievement that a student receives in programmed learning and his knowledge of his accomplishment enhance the motivation of the learner and may make the act of learning intrinsically rewarding." Wow!

One of the problems raised by these students was that the *machine* did not allow them to go back to review their work.

This is a problem that is gradually being resolved. The Min-Max II, for example, makes provision for the student to take out frames that have been used, if he wants to review some of the questions or subject matter that have already gone before.

But there's a question, as Theodore Waller points out: How much looking back should be permitted? Here we come upon the old argument of whether children should be allowed to look ahead, or look back, or not. The issue of cheating arises. If children can fill out their answers, and then look back, they will get the correct answers.

This problem does not exist in most of the non-machine programmed instruction materials now being used, points out Dr. Maurice Mitchell. Children can go forward or backward at their own pace and without feeling guilty. They are not warned to "answer one frame at a time." It really doesn't matter, since they are not graded on their day to day work. They are graded at the end of each week or semester, or by some other arrangement made with the teacher.

Actually, most programs build in a certain amount of review work in each course. In algebra 2, for example, the early material in the course may be a review of algebra 1. The teacher's guide on testing, for algebra 2, in the Temac course says: "The entire class can take the first few tests at the same time. Some members of the class may need to spend extra time outside the classroom on the programmed material whereas others may have free time in the classroom to review or to do supplementary work."

The question of review is one that has not been fully or satisfactorily answered. But here, too, the program builders are working on the problem. They know that review is important. They know, also, that it is much easier to build reviews in programmed instruction than in the machines themselves.

In summary, these are the conclusions I reached after my interviews with students:

1. Most students prefer teaching machines to the methods of the conventional classroom.

2. They would rather have both the machine and the human teacher than either one alone.

3. They feel that a human teacher is especially important in discussion subjects such as social studies, philosophy, creative writing, and history—in brief, the non-tool subjects.

4. They think the teaching machine needs to be improved so that it can allow for review. In order to get a firm grasp on a subject, they want at times to be able to go over material they've already studied.

5. Students respond enthusiastically to immediate reinforcement.

6. They believe the step-by-step framing technique helps them learn better.

7. They like the principle of errorless learning.

8. They like being able to study at their own pace and accept this opportunity as a challenge rather than as a shield for laziness.

9. They believe programmed learning is especially suited to the bright student and the student who is below average.

10. In all their comments about the machine's patience, its adjustment to individual differences, its technique of small steps and rewards, the students made a very definite response in favor of the new learning psychology and against the aversive psychology of the traditional classroom.

CHAPTER FIVE

How Do Teachers React?

I suppose the very first question we should deal with in this chapter is:

Can teaching machines replace teachers?

My own answer is "No." There is much more to education than the embedding of facts in young minds—which is what a machine does supremely well. But no machine can relate ideas with the sudden, almost breathtaking insight that drives them deep into the personality of a student and makes them live. This is what a good teacher does, and if we can judge by their remarks in the last chapter, students know this and want it. A great deal of what we call education is simply learning by example. Wisdom, after all, is not the influence of ideas on machines but on people. A teacher can be an unforgettable example of wisdom; a machine can't.

That is my personal answer to the question, and it puts me in agreement with some educators and in disagreement with others.

In this chapter we will repeat many educators' remarks, in

quote or paraphrase. Let's begin with Dr. Francis Keppel, Dean of the Graduate School of Education at Harvard. During a visit I had with him, he said, "I'll accept the machine as a replacement for a teacher when it can run a birthday party for my young daughter, when it can comfort a sick child or encourage a child who needs reassurance. Then I'll go along with the idea that a machine is as good as a teacher."

Dr. Sidney L. Pressey, the "grandfather" of the new technique, assures us that "it is a mistake to think of machines as Frankenstein monsters replacing present-day texts, methods, and even teachers. Rather, this new device should be the greatest help teachers ever had." Here Dr. Pressey gives us one of the most common arguments in favor of machines: they will release the teacher from routine drudgery (hours spent in grading tests, reiterating the most basic facts) and free him for a creative role (giving attention to individual children and provoking interest in ideas the machine can't teach).

This same point was stated not as argument but as fact by Dr. James J. Asher, an associate professor of statistics at San Jose State College in California. "What excites me about programmed learning," he said, "is that it frees me from the role of drill-master. The program drills the student, at home, in an almost painless step-by-step procedure, so that when he comes to class he is ready to apply statistical ideas to actual research problems. What this means is that I now have the time to help each student with his own unique difficulties. Every undergraduate in the statistics class gets the attention and guidance usually reserved only for graduate students."

For many years Dr. T. W. Blyth of Hamilton College has been teaching a course in logic. He finds that giving his class programmed instruction to take home saves him a great deal of time formerly wasted on routine checking or drill. Instead of holding classes for three hours a week, he now meets with students for only two and still covers more material than he could with conventional methods. He also finds the new technique enables him to pinpoint a student's problems very quickly by checking his answers on the program. As a result, he can teach more quickly and with greater effectiveness. Moreover, since the students get the concepts and principles of their course at home, the class time can be devoted to the development of these concepts and their applications to new areas.

Another teacher told me, "I found that by using English 2600 (a programmed grammar text), I was able to devote more time in the classroom to literature and composition. I let the students use it on a self-help basis. They got along without me but we all agreed later that the time we spent discussing literature gave them a better understanding of the English language."

"So far I'm very happy with programmed instruction," said Glenn Spieg, an algebra teacher at South Side High School in Rockville Centre, New York. "Students don't get bored when they go at a speed that is natural to them. If I'm out for a day or if they're home sick, we don't have to make up for lost time. They can go right ahead at their own pace. I have 28 pupils and could easily handle many more."

Here are some more brief but typical comments:

"I now have more time to spend with students who are having trouble."

"Machines give me a chance to prepare a more thorough curriculum. I've been able to work in many more anecdotes and examples for my social studies course than I could before."

"The teaching machine lets me use a tutorial system, which previously would have been impossible in a class of 38."

"I like the machines because they take care of the talented

students. Before, the children who knew the work would often sit back and wait with almost patronizing looks on their faces while I drummed information into the heads of the duller students."

William Fullagar, Dean of the University of Rochester College of Education, points out that "the principles of learning in programmed instruction are simply those which the best teachers try to apply in the classroom."

Finally, Dr. Skinner, writing for *Science:* "Will machines replace the teacher? On the contrary, they are capital equipment to be used by teachers to save time and labor. In assigning certain mechanizable functions to the machines, the teacher emerges in his proper role as an indispensable human being. He may teach more students than heretofore, which is inevitable if the worldwide demand for education is to be satisfied, but he will do so in fewer hours and with fewer burdensome chores. In return for his greater productivity, he can hope to improve his economic condition."

The gist of all these arguments, prophesies, and assertions of fact is this: machines will not make an anachronism of the teacher, but will free him for his own education—travel, reading, writing or research—as well as for those creative tasks of instruction and guidance which are the core of his profession. Through the years I have heard scores of teachers express variations of a common theme: "If only I had less paper work! If only I didn't have to do so many non-teaching jobs. I would really like the time to teach!" To these teachers, programmed learning holds a promise and potential I don't think has been seen before in American education. It will help eliminate the vast amount of their non-teaching work, although of course, the non-teaching unprofessional jobs of the classroom (like collecting milk money) will not be eliminated completely.

Teachers will be better able, with freer time, to concentrate on the task at hand, that of becoming master teachers. Those who have experimented with the teaching machine found that their daily drudgery was greatly eliminated.

A Vigorous Debate

As I have suggested, however, there is another opinion of programmed learning which takes its cue from the kind of remark made by Dr. Norman Crowder, the inventor of scrambled books. Referring to his branching technique, he said, "This type of program enables a student to learn without the aid of a teacher."

Dr. Maurice W. Sullivan, former director of graduate studies in foreign languages at Hollins College, Roanoke, puts the case against teachers in its most extreme form. "I think we can program every subject there is," he said. "I would even go a step further. I think we could do without teachers. And I would go to a step beyond that. I think the school of the future will be in the home and not in public school buildings. A teacher might be available for supervision but the student with his machine in his home would be able to do the same kind of work that he can do in the classroom today."

In support of Dr. Sullivan's contention, a class which was organized without a teacher at Roanoke did just as well as a class that had a teacher in it. Again, in Pittsburgh, high school physics students performed as well without a teacher as with one. Other studies at the college level suggest there are instances in which machines can be at least as effective as teachers.

Not long ago an upstate New York community bought 20 machines for classroom installation. The newspapers headlined the event with predictions that teachers were about to become things of the past. One economy-minded citizen wrote a letter to the editor saying, in effect: "Wonderful! Those 20 machines are a good omen. This fall we can get rid of 20 teachers!" It wasn't a remark to warm the cockles of teachers' hearts.

In Utah, the *Salt Lake City Tribune* printed this little obituary of a sort: "The first Utah teacher already has been shouldered aside by a machine. He is a mathematics teacher at Weber County High School, and Superintendent T. H. Bell assigned him to a junior high school next fall.

"His place at Weber will be taken by an automated teaching machine and the materials it uses.

" 'Using 60 of these machines, one teacher can handle six classes of 60 students each, or 360 students a day in algebra and trigonometry,' Supt. Bell said. 'Each of the two high schools in the district will be equipped next fall with 120 machines, and two teachers in each school will thus be able to handle up to 720 students daily.' "

Bigger classes, even when buttressed by machines, do not appeal to many teachers. One teacher told me: "Look, I have 33 pupils now and I can't give them the attention they need. Do you expect me to take 60? No sir! I just won't do it."

"The worst aspects of mass education can be seen in oversized classes," another teacher said. "It's preposterous to say we can handle as many as 60 students, machines or no."

Still another: "The idea of being replaced by a machine just infuriates me."

To which a skeptic said: "Any teacher who can be replaced by a machine shouldn't be in school."

"Why don't you like the teaching machine?" I asked a high school teacher of English. "Have you ever tried it?"

"No," she answered belligerently. "I've been teaching for 35 years and I won't have a machine tell me what to do!"

This teacher is watching the reactions of her elementary school students carefully as they use Min-Max teaching machines.

"But," I replied, "no one has ever said that the machine will boss you around. You'll be the boss. Maybe it'll take some of the chores out of teaching and give you more time to be creative."

"Stuff and nonsense," she snorted. "I'm creative enough as it is. Besides, I'm scared stiff of any kind of machine or gadget."

Many of these first reactions are heavily laden with emotion, as is only natural in a climate of extravagant claims for programmed learning. All that can be said at this early date is that machines appear to pose a greater threat to the teacher of tool subjects than to the teacher of humanities. Even in mathematics, languages, and sciences, however, it is by no means certain that machines can completely replace teachers. Much more research will have to be undertaken before the answers stand out with any clarity.

"I sympathize with those teachers who are apprehensive about teaching machines," says Dr. David G. Salten, superintendent of schools in Long Beach, N.Y. "The problem is very complex and it bears on our whole administrative structure. Before it is resolved we will have to think through the serious question of retraining our teachers."

Dr. Frederick M. Raubinger, New Jersey commissioner of education, told me he was not opposed to anything that would make a teacher more effective, but he insisted that the teacher must be the judge of when, whether, and to what extent any kind of classroom aid should be used. "It is incredible to me," he said, "that teaching machines have not been subjected to closer scrutiny by the profession and the public."

So there you have it—a big question mark. Amidst the more heated and irrational claims being pressed by both sides in the debate, a great deal of serious research is going on. Eventually it will settle the question "Can machines replace teachers?" to the teachers' satisfaction. My sympathies, as the very existence of this book suggests, lie with a hopeful future for the teaching machine—a future in which the human teacher is as firmly entrenched as he is today and freer to pursue his larger tasks than he has ever been.

Let us get one thing straight: the teaching machine will never fully replace the teacher. It is not a threat. Just as progressive education freed the child from a hostile, stuffy climate, so the teaching machine will free the teacher from drudgery and routine work.

The new technological age cannot be swept under the rug. It is here to stay.

Another big question teacher asks is: Aren't there flaws in the teaching machines?

Flaws? Certainly, just as there were in the Model T Ford, or in Orville and Wilbur Wright's first flying machine. Here are some of the disadvantages of teaching machines, as outlined by a representative group of teachers:

1. Students occasionally complain of boredom. They say they get bored sitting in front of a machine all day, without active contact with classmates and teacher.

2. Some of the children cheat, look ahead in their books, skip over the hard questions and appear indifferent.

3. Some of the students are not able to work independently. They constantly fall back upon the teacher for spoon-feeding; they end up being inadequately prepared.

4. Some students lack genuine understanding or appreciation of the subject.

Programmers and machine builders are not closing their eyes and ears to these complaints, justified or not, but are working full speed to improve machines and programs.

Retraining Teachers

This much *is* certain: teachers have to be convinced that programmed learning is a good thing or it will never work. In a study conducted by Encyclopaedia Britannica Films at Roanoke, it was found that when teachers were hostile to machines, the students did poorly. They seemed to recognize a lack of enthusiasm on the part of their instructors. Because of this, I would not like to see machines introduced into any school system which had not prepared its teachers for them in advance.

"The teacher has a vital role to play in programmed instruction," says E.B.F.'s Dr. Allen D. Calvin. "A sympathetic and well informed teacher is even more important to a programmed course than to a conventional one."

Dr. Clifford Rall, superintendent of schools in Port Chester, New York, has given considerable thought to the same problem: "I would never use a teacher in programmed instruction unless she was sympathetic to this method of teaching."

Teachers agree that the student is helped. Actually, the principles of programmed learning are those which the best teachers try to apply in the classroom.

Fortunately, it has been found that most teachers lose their antagonism to machines once they have used them. Sometimes this process takes place quickly, sometimes it takes months. In a few cases, of course, it doesn't occur at all. Obviously we can't expect teachers with 20 or 25 years of experience to forget methods it has taken them a whole career to refine.

What is called for, I think, is a broad retraining program for teachers who are now on the job, and a thorough training of prospective teachers who are enrolled in colleges of education. Of the 2,000,000 teachers in our school system, both on the private and public level, it is unlikely that more than 100,000 have had any experience with teaching machines. As programmed learning gains currency, we must find ways to acquaint the remaining 1,900,000 with its methods. This might be done best during the off-months of the summer. I think it would also be desirable to offer courses on teaching machines in programmed form. If teachers learned about the new educational psychology through its own techniques, they would be better equipped to teach it to their students.

While all this training and retraining is taking place, programmers and manufacturers of teaching machines will have to refine their product. Thus far only a small number of psychologists are at work on programmed learning. Few as they are, however, they have quite often operated at cross-purposes. Until they resolve some of their more emotional differences of opinion, they will have a hard time convincing teachers they are on the right track. Sloppy, ineffective programs must be kept from reaching the schools, for they can only result in disillusionment among educators.

At this stage, however, the prospects for general acceptance of programmed learning are good. In my survey of some 50 teachers who are using machines or self-tutoring books, I found only 10 per cent of them were opposed to the new technique, 10 per cent were undecided about it, and 80 per cent favored it wholeheartedly.

Solving the Teacher Shortage

America faces an almost overwhelming shortage of teachers. Even by conservative estimate we already need 150,000 more teachers than we have. Within ten years that figure will jump to 750,000 for our elementary and secondary schools and 250,000 for our colleges—a total of 1,000,000. It is quite obvious that we just aren't going to be able to train enough teachers to fill the bill, especially with 11 per cent of our teaching force leaving the profession every year.

There is one heartening thing about these statistics, however: they are based on the conventional classroom size of 30 or so students. What would happen if this number rose to 45, with no impairment of educational quality? Surely the dearth of teachers would be much reduced.

It has been demonstrated that the new machines enable the teacher to handle up to twice as many students as before. By

Programming is the subject we are discussing with James Evans, head of programming for Teaching Machines, Inc., in Albuquerque.

relieving her of much paperwork and simple rote education, they give her both the time and control she needs to deal with a larger classroom. Teaching machines may consequently prove to be the greatest single remedy for the shortage of teachers in the next decade.

We can safely venture one other prediction: with a need for 1,000,000 more teachers by 1972, programmed learning can pose no threat to the profession as a whole. It may cause some dislocations in the tool subjects, but it will be the job of retraining programs to make the transition from old to new methods as smooth as possible. Eventually, as with all technological advances, a great number of new jobs will be called into existence. We will need skilled programmers. Since machines have a way of pointing up individual differences, we will need thousands of guidance counselors who are trained to deal with students who have taken programmed instruction. Guidance counselors will find it essential to recognize the importance of teaching machines, and convey this knowledge to parents and students alike. They will have to explain why one student may finish a year's course in geometry in one month, for example, and another will take a whole year; also, the same student may take twice as long as a parent thinks he should take in a programmed course in grammar.

More than that, guidance counselors will have to guide to college, seniors who have spent varying lengths of time in completing their high school courses—some four years, some $3\frac{1}{2}$ years, some three, or even less. This will cause counselors to work more closely with college admission officers to explain their school's particular course of programmed instruction.

Whether handling old jobs or creating new ones, the machine will have a salutary economic effect on the teaching profession.

Programmed Class Organization

Teaching machines are bound to change the structure of American classrooms, both in school and college. We don't know what their ultimate impact will be, but we are hardly prepared to go along with Dr. Sullivan in his statement that we can do without teachers, and that the school of the future will be in the home. He has, however, given us an inkling of one future extreme.

In such a boldly imagined system, students might study at home and take exams which would be graded at a national center of programmed learning. Curricula in the liberal arts, sciences, mechanical arts, and most other fields would all be planned at the center, and the center would also award degrees and organize field trips, on-the-job training, and other necessary adjuncts to basic education.

Since national control of education is an idea which rubs against the grain of American traditions, the new system might better be administered locally. In this event, the student would study at home and report to a community center for testing and guidance. The problems inherent in both schemes are so vast as to make them almost implausibly difficult to achieve. Nevertheless the revolutionary idea proposed by Dr. Sullivan is worth thinking about. Extreme as it is, it may stimulate more realizable schemes and serve as a kind of radical measuring rod for them.

At the very least, programmed learning will alter the size of modern classrooms and rearrange the timing and methods of instruction. Rooms will hold from five students to 200, depending on the course. In tool subjects, where there is little need for informal discussion, the classes will be large and run almost entirely by machine. They will probably not require teachers as we now think of them, but will make use of instructors who are skilled in the mechanics of particular machines and programs. These instructors will issue and grade tests and help students over rough spots in the programmed courses. If the machines are electronic, the instructor may exert some control over them through a push-button console on his desk.

In the humanities, such as literature and history, classes will probably be smaller, although they too may run as high as 100 students. Part of the time will be devoted to lectures and discussion, the rest to study on the machines. In this latter portion, there is no organic class as such, because each student is moving at his own pace. If there are 75 students, there will really be 75 separate classes.

This will create an immense organizational problem. If, in a typical class of eighth-grade algebra students, 10 per cent finish the year's work in four months, and 50 per cent in six months, where are they going to spend the rest of the school year? Are they to be started on the next subject or given additional work in their current one? What use are lectures and group discussions when every student has reached a different stage in the program?

Carrying the thought still further, will it be possible for gifted pupils to finish grammar, junior, and senior high school in four years and enter Harvard at the age of 10? What will happen to social life for teen-agers?

The school of the future—and it may well be a grammar, junior, and senior high school all wrapped into one—will be concerned with one goal: the education of each student according to his individual talents. If this means abolishing classes as we now know them, so be it. Horizontal grade levels with all students approximately the same age may disappear. The present grading system may cease to exist as differences in test scores become less noticeable than differences in the time needed to finish any given course. If a student can raise a B to an A with the use of a teaching machine, or an F to a C, grades become meaningless.

Colleges may have to revise their admissions standards to handle a situation in which 75 per cent of their candidates are "A" students. In all of these dislocations and shifts of emphasis, the teacher's role is bound to change. Rather than teach one subject simultaneously to 30, 50, or 100 students, he may act more as a guidance counselor who prepares a separate curriculum for each student. With college or career in mind, he might send his students off to a library cubicle or room equipped with machines, and at varying intervals give them tests, special assignments, and new programs of study.

The library and the school librarian will also feel the impact of machine learning. For one thing, the library will become a reservoir of information about teaching machines. No single journal has yet been published which deals exclusively or even adequately with programs and machines. Eventually, however, this kind of publication will come into existence. In the meantime, many isolated articles on programmed instruction will appear in different magazines and newspapers. The librarian will have to keep up with this increasing flow of information and organize it in such a way that it can be quickly tapped by teachers, superintendents, and other school personnel.

The library will also be a center of programmed learning. It will be stocked with self-tutoring books and programs for machines. It will undoubtedly be equipped with machines themselves, suitable for a wide variety of programmed courses and numerous enough to handle the army of students that programmed learning will send through the doors of the library.

In a recent article in *The Library Journal*, Mr. Waller pointed out that the chief effect of the teaching machine on school libraries will inevitably be to bring the latter closer to the teacher and the student. The teacher may wish to have the students use the time saved through use of the machines for supplementary reading. Teachers are expected to send many students to the library to work on additional projects. A student who may finish his programmed course in French, may be assigned readings in French literature or history, or begin a programmed course in Spanish or Italian.

The student who regards the librarian as someone who helps him only when he has a dull assignment or to while away hours on a rainy day may become aware of this new development in education.

"The librarian, in cooperation with the teacher, will be even more active in developing specialized supplementary reading lists," Mr. Waller said.

No one can predict what the school of 1975 will be like, what function the new classroom will serve, or what the teacher's role will be. All I can say for certain is that teaching machines now confront us with a vast challenge and immense possibilities of change. The next decade is going to be an interesting one for American education.

CHAPTER SIX

What Can Teaching Machines Teach?

Like most of the issues surrounding teaching machines, the question of *what* they can teach provoked a variety of clashing answers. On the one hand we have the enthusiastic reply of Dr. Sullivan.

"Machines can teach anything," he said. "I don't see why they can't handle every subject there is."

Dr. Skinner, too, claims, "Anything that can be verbalized can be taught in a teaching machine."

Most educators, however, would be more inclined to go along with Dean Keppel. "There are definite limitations to the number of courses that can be taught with teaching machines," he said. "They cannot teach those subjects that require interpretation and insight."

There you have the differences of opinion.

No one yet knows the full range of the wonderful teaching-machine device. But we do know it isn't narrow. Temple University recently issued a bulletin which listed 130 courses of programmed instruction including algebra, arithmetic, book-keeping, calculus, chemistry, economics, electricity, English, French, geometry, German, Latin, law, photography, physics, psychology, reading, Russian, Spanish, spelling, statistics, trigonometry, and vocabulary development.

"Tool" Subjects

So far the greatest value of teaching machines appears to lie in "tool" subjects in the fields of mathematics, science, and language which deal with measurements, rules, or natural laws. It is possible to analyze finite information into small fractions of knowledge which are ideal for the framing technique of a program. Machines can grapple with facts, but they cannot teach imagination, emotional or artistic sensitivity, or the intellectual insight which relates widely different ideas. Dr. Skinner has developed a program to help a student memorize a long poem but he has not yet found one which will teach a student to enjoy poetry!

There are other limitations. Programmed learning is one-dimensional and linear, whether the line is straight as in a Skinner text or scrambled as in one of Crowder's books. How can it teach a course in American history which must deal three-dimensionally with events, people, ideas, and the subtle relationships among them? Or how would an English teacher use a machine if she wanted to give an overall view of the changes that brought about the Elizabethan Age? These subjects are not strictly analytical. It's difficult to see how they could be adequately programmed. Of course, Dr. Sullivan would disagree with me. So would Mr. Waller, who believes programmed instruction can teach subjects as intangible as composition.

Perhaps history, writing, philosophy, and other non-tool

subjects could be taught by separating the functions of human and mechanical teachers. Machines would handle the simpler ideas and basic facts, such as dates, events, and rules; the human teacher would then relate these facts and give them meaning. Until this is done, however, teaching machines will have their greatest influence on more factual subjects.

Reading Skill

In Albuquerque I saw the excitement of youngsters from 4 to 6 years of age who were being taught to read through programmed instruction. They enjoyed what they were doing and looked forward to each new frame with enthusiasm. Moreover, they could stop when they wanted to without dropping behind the rest of their class. As a battalion of students marching at a single speed, the class did not exist; it was merely a spatial arrangement of many youngsters who were moving at many different rates through a reading course.

I watched little 5-year-olds learning to read words which normally appear only in the first or second grade. Their machines taught them to recognize letters simply as visual patterns, whether capitals or lower-case, written or printed. When phonographic attachments were added to the machines, the youngsters quickly learned to associate sounds with patterns.

Much more work will have to be done in programmed reading, but what I have seen convinces me that this is a valuable avenue of exploration. Educators who have used the machines believe they can teach reading in half the time and with half the effort required by a human teacher with conventional textbooks.

In a closely allied field, spelling, Dr. Douglas Porter of Harvard experimented with second-, fourth-, and sixth-grade children and found they learned much more efficiently with machines than with traditional methods.

Languages

Federal funds under the National Defense Education Act have enabled many schools to build audio and audio-visual devices which are very useful in teaching foreign languages. These devices don't always contain the full program we have been talking about, but they do provide one of Dr. Skinner's chief aids to learning: immediate reinforcement.

I visited a mechanized class in German whose machine

This man is learning Chinese on U.S. Industry, Inc.'s MemoTutor.

pronounces words as they flash on a screen. The student then articulates the words himself. His speech is recorded on tape, which he re-plays to hear how closely his accent matches the correct one.

I went into the booth and tried the machine. I put on earphones and pressed a button. "Guten morgen," the voice said, "guten nacht . . . Good morning, good evening." I repeated the words, listened to my own voice, and by the end of 15 minutes had mastered a number of other German phrases.

The combination of visual images, sounds, and immediate reinforcement teaches efficiently and pleasantly.

The day is not far off when all languages will be taught in this way. Already the teaching machine, in conjunction with audio-visual aids, the tape recorder and the television screen, have made language laboratories commonplace in our schools and colleges. Nothing like this has ever happened before in the history of American education. We now have a completely new method of teaching foreign languages.

Science

Most natural sciences can be programmed. A very fine example is an introductory course in psychology offered by Dr. James Holland at Harvard. Among the topics covered were reflexes, Pavlovian conditioning, motivation, techniques of personal control, and behavioristic analysis of psychotherapy.

Ten machines, sufficient for 187 students, last year handled about one-third of the teaching, which also included outside reading and lectures. The students were free to use the machine room whenever they wished. One student completed the entire semester of 48 program discs in two all-day sessions. Those taking the course found the work enjoyable and said their grasp of the subject was stronger than it would have been without the machines.

Inasmuch as the sciences are growing in unexpected ways every year, it is important to keep teaching and courses up to date. Said Dr. Holland, "One of the best things about the machines is that they allow us to make constant year-to-year revisions of material. We can adjust programs to the students' behavior and keep up with new discoveries in any field." The teaching machine is ideally suited to this subject.

Assorted Subjects

You already know that almost anything from arithmetic to zoology can be drafted into a program. Some programmed subjects may nevertheless surprise you.

At a recent workshop in Pittsburgh under the auspices of the American Institute for Research, Dr. Klaus introduced a course on English money. (This was prior to the disclosure that the English government was planning to adopt a decimal currency.) Similar programs, dealing with geography, currency, customs, and useful phrases, could be made into booklets for Americans travelling in foreign countries. They would be quite inexpensive; the programmed material on English money sells for only fifty cents.

Teaching Materials Corporation has developed a program which teaches music. This self-tutoring book may not give rise to any new Brahms or Beethovens, but it does give students a clear idea of harmony, rhythm, melody, and other musical elements. Of course, the student will still have to flail away at his piano or guitar. The book won't do that for him. There are machines, however, that can sharpen a student's sense of pitch and make his ear sensitive to intervals between notes. Naturally, these machines are audio devices. Some of them are hooked up to small piano keyboards. A live instructor sitting at a console plays a chord, and the student is asked to reproduce it on the piano.

These are only some of the many unusual subjects that can be taught by teaching machines. Moving away from education in its formal aspects, we might note that such home-oriented activities as gardening and chess and contract bridge are ideal for programming. We begin to see that programmed learning has a tremendous future outside as well as inside the basic school system.

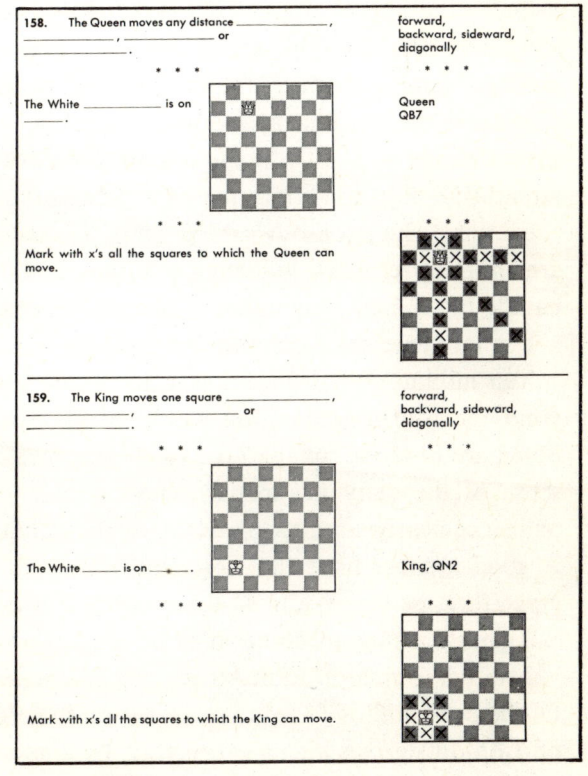

Page from E.B.F. program called "The Game of Chess."

158. The Queen moves any distance _____, _____, _____ or _____.
· · ·
The White _____ is on _____.
Queen QB7
· · ·
Mark with x's all the squares to which the Queen can move.
forward, backward, sideward, diagonally
· · ·

159. The King moves one square _____, _____, _____ or _____.
· · ·
The White _____ is on _____.
King, QN2
· · ·
Mark with x's all the squares to which the King can move.
forward, backward, sideward, diagonally
· · ·

37 *The Game of Chess*

Teaching Machines and Adult Education

It may well be that the biggest beneficiaries of programmed learning will be the immense and varied group of people who study part-time. Roughly four million American adults are taking courses sponsored by their local public schools. Another six million are enrolled in university extension courses or programs of unions, companies, communities, the Red Cross, Y.M.C.A. and Y.W.C.A.

The largest adult enrollment is in trade, business, and technical subjects. Next in popularity is general education, which includes the liberal arts of history, language, philosophy, and literature. Ranking third are courses for the family: child care, sewing, home economics, interior decorating, and financing.

Despite the enrollment figures, are public schools meeting the challenge of adult education? No, not always. Adults who attend school in the afternoon or evening often get a slipshod education. The drop-out rate is preposterously high. Schools are short of teachers, guidance counselors, and supervisors to handle the tremendous influx of after-hours students.

I believe teaching machines can take up the slack.

Ten million American adults who cannot read or write beyond the fourth-grade level never go to after-hours school. Some are illiterate, unable to scrawl their own names or make sense of the daily newspaper. These people do not lack intelligence nearly so much as they lack the opportunity to learn. A good number have superior minds. Their illiteracy is a disgrace to America. We must teach them, but how?

Again, teaching machines may be the answer.

Another 67 million adult Americans did not finish high school. Of these, 44 million failed to reach the ninth grade. The number of drop-outs grows higher every year. No one will quarrel with the statement that the United States owes every one of its citizens at least a high school education. But how are we going to educate people who are busy working or supporting families? They no longer have time for formal study.

Teaching machines can educate them.

We know that adults out of school, as well as youngsters in school, often lack the proper motivation to learn. Teaching machines have a freshness and an unorthodoxy that are bound to create enthusiasm. Moreover, as we have seen, programmed learning makes use of the natural human desire for rewards, creates its own motivation, makes learning easy and cuts study time. Every one of these qualities is perfectly tailored for the education of adults.

There are a number of ways that teaching machines can be introduced into adult education: through direct company-to-home sales of programmed books and machines; through programmed correspondence courses; through programmed study at, or by borrowing from, local libraries; and through after-hours courses at schools and colleges.

As machines gain the acceptance they surely must, adults will eventually be able to study almost any subject on a teaching machine or in a self-tutoring book.

Every year millions of people enroll in courses through the mails. I would not be surprised if nearly all correspondence subjects now taught by traditional methods were eventually offered in program form.

A harbinger of the coming change is the program for U.S. census-takers now being developed by Dr. Klaus. In 1960 it took 16 hours to train each of 160,000 men and women for the census. Dr. Klaus estimates the new programmed correspondence course will do the job in half the time, with a big financial saving for the government.

The public libraries which serve an estimated 100 million Americans every year could become centers of programmed learning. When they recognize this fact, they'll lend machines, programs, and self-tutoring books as they now lend ordinary books, films, records, and art.

Between 1939 and 1956, enrollment in adult classes at elementary and secondary schools jumped from two to three million. The figure has risen by another million in just the last five years. Additional thousands of adults are taking part-time courses at colleges and universities. This vast, immensely important phase of education is made sluggish by the lack of teachers and the cumbersome methods of the traditional classroom. Moreover, adults often cannot find sufficient time for study; their families and jobs take precedence over education.

It is obvious what we must do: teach adults in less time than previously, and with less reliance on the overburdened human teacher. In short, we must educate them through programmed instruction. The new adult classroom may contain 60, 70, or 100 machines and one instructor. From time to time the instructor will give a lecture, but more often he will simply lend direction to the course, answer questions, and supervise tests. When they are not in class, the part-time students can do homework on machines of their own or with self-tutoring books. Adult education will thus be made faster, cleaner, and more enjoyable. Programmed learning will untangle much of the logistical clutter in the schools, while its underlying psychology will encourage thousands of Americans to renew the process of education which, regardless of one's age, is never complete.

Suggestions for the Future

Why not program courses such as television repairing, mechanics and plumbing? Then offer them through trade schools, labor unions and other agencies?

Which brings another thought: why not self-teaching centers? Devices and programs could be made available to learners on a rental basis.

Far fetched? No. Dr. Lloyd Morrisett, executive assistant of the Carnegie Corporation, calls teaching machines a natural for home study. Many adults, he observes, may want to take machine correspondence courses, or refresher courses to keep up with new fields.

Properly programmed teaching-machine courses are the best hope for extension of adult education. Parents should keep up with new school problems. Voters want to know about vital international issues. Citizens everywhere are concerned with war and peace, bombs and fall-out shelters, Cuba and Communism, Indonesia and Red China.

Go back to school and learn about these issues? Most of us won't. Learn about them at home? Most of us will.

Of greatest interest to adults will be the time saved. The teaching machine cuts the time to master a subject by 50 per cent, or, as in the case of medical technology, as much as 75 per cent. When one is 18, time doesn't mean much. But at 48, time rushes past rapidly.

"I would like to learn Russian," a middle-aged financier told me the other day, "but I'm too old. I don't have that many years left."

Maybe the teaching machine is the answer.

Lawrence M. Stolurow in a study made for the U.S. Office of Education found that college students, military trainees and adults generally did better work and had a more rapid learning rate than those studying in the traditional manner. Dr. Stolurow notes: "In a wide variety of contexts, with several different kinds of subject matter, and with adults of varying levels of ability, it appears that knowledge of results, if implemented in a fairly consistent and systematic manner, is likely to have important educational and training benefits. The teaching machine seems to be a major breakthrough in education, comparable to the book, radio and television."

Strong language? Yes. But I will go along with the above findings. The teaching machine is in a position to change the theory of teaching.

Teaching Machines and Industry

The demand for teaching machines is growing fast in business and industry. It's easy to understand why.

Manufacturers spend approximately $100 million a year in formal training of employees. Courses range from elementary subjects to those of an advanced technical or professional nature, and they are given to executives as well as laborers. Professor Harold S. Clark of Teachers College at Columbia University estimates that industrial training accounts for two-thirds of the money spent on the entire educational system in the U.S. every year.

Industry has found many basic job skills can be programmed, such as manipulation of tools, blueprint reading, names of parts, shop mathematics, radio code instruction, shorthand, and typing. Hundreds of other routine tasks, from meter reading to assembly-line inspection, could be successfully programmed.

Firms that make expensive products requiring exact workmanship could benefit from teaching machines. Programmed learning is especially useful for those industries which have a rapid technological change, for they are unlikely to find skilled personnel in new fields of operation. More probably, they must retrain old workers for the new jobs.

Teaching machines are also natural money-savers for companies whose investment per worker is high. Their employees are highly skilled; consequently it takes a lot of money and time to train them. Although their skills are sophisticated, they deal with the kind of hard fact that is ideal for programmed learning. The time now spent in training these workers could be cut in half (see page 127), with a respectable lessening of costs, if teaching machines were used. I don't see how airlines, for instance, now devoting thousands of dollars to the training of pilots, maintenance crews, and flight controllers, can fail to recognize the advantages of this new educational technique.

Bell Telephone, Eastman Kodak, and Westinghouse are among the large companies which have already introduced or are planning to introduce teaching machines in their training programs. It took a Kodak programmer 40 hours to develop a trial course in logarithms, but the company recovered the expense of his time after only two groups had gone through the course. Like all good programs, it engrossed the learner's attention from start to finish. "This machine really means business," one worker told me.

Hughes Aircraft has installed a device called "Videosonic" which has most of the characteristics of a teaching machine. Women working on three assembly lines are given step-by-step instruction through earphones and television. The new training system has worked remarkably well. Hughes reports that the number of rejected assemblies has dropped by 70 per cent. The company has also been able to operate with fewer supervisors and inspectors.

Polaroid has programmed courses in mathematics and physics for its employees. Some flaws have become apparent, however; a few students grow restless and bored, while others say the program is too slow. Polaroid is not yet convinced that learning from programmed material is retained as well as material traditionally taught.

International Business Machines has begun a programmed course for its service personnel and customers. The new course has already allowed it to cut training time from 15 to 8 weeks. One interesting fact now evident in the I.B.M. operation is that machines and programmed books seem to work equally well.

In Little Falls, N.J., I visited the plant of General Precision Company. The firm makes an inertial-guidance system which can guide several missiles at a time without ground control. Its parts must be accurate to 1/50,000 of an inch. This company, like many others, has developed an excellent training program for its assembly workers, repair shop personnel, field engineers, and customers. The program consists of administrative subjects and 28 courses in avionics—the science which deals with inertial guidance systems.

I spoke with employees who had taken some of the courses on teaching machines. They all said they enjoyed the new kind of training and found it effective. Herbert Ivens, superintendent of the service shop, made a typical comment:

"The machine taught me a lot of things I didn't know," he said. "It brought back information I had forgotten long ago, too. My work began to make much more sense after a course in electronics. The best thing about the teaching machine seems to be that it keeps the men alert, on their toes. They learn about twice as fast and don't get bored. Sometimes a guy who has been around a while resents being taught something new by another employee, but there's never any resistance to a machine."

One of Ivens' remarks was particularly significant: machines are perfectly tailored to bridge the gap between what has been learned in college and what must be practiced in business or industry. This fact was supported by a young college graduate who is taking a refresher course in calculus on the teaching machine.

"Although I got an A in calculus in college, I was never taught how to apply it to what I'm doing now," he told me. "The factory gives me two hours a week off so I can use the machine. In about ten weeks I'll be ready for a higher paying job."

So far the greatest drawback to programmed learning in industry has been the scarcity of programs. There are other problems, such as a rate of technological change that quickly makes old methods obsolete. What is needed, I think, is an institute which would prepare, check, and update all programs used in industry, or at least those programs for which there is a wide demand. (Specialized manufacturers would still have to develop their own training subjects.) This institute would foster the close cooperation of factory training officials, psychologists, and specialists in whatever fields were to be taught. It would make programmed learning a vital, coherent process in American industry.

Teaching Machines and National Defense

More experiments are being conducted with teaching machines in the armed forces than in any other area, not excluding industry and formal education. The services now spend $600 million a year for training. Their interest in mechanical teaching aids is not new. During World War II, I visited camps where the Army was using advanced audio- and visual-instruction devices. The Army had perfected a six-week program at that time which gave the equivalent of four years' education to men who had not reached the fifth grade. Almost two decades before the present boom in programmed learning, the services recognized and exploited the benefits of allowing students to learn at different speeds.

Today, teaching machines are helping our armed forces train thousands of men in the use of the complicated weapons and machinery of modern warfare. The Air Force now teaches electronics, electricity, mechanics, and many other subjects by machine.

Because the services must deal with hundreds of thousands of men, the machines they require are generally large electronic audio-visual devices. These machines likewise require programmers to develop a far-ranging catalogue of courses.

The armed services *are* developing teaching-machine programs to fit their own needs. So far, they have utilized general training devices, have not concentrated on individual techniques, and have focused on methods to train particular skills required to maintain complex equipment systems.

In some of the military experiments teaching machines have replaced teachers altogether.

An Army technical sergeant told me why he preferred to work with teaching machines: "The machine is patient," he said. "It never scolds or is sarcastic. It helps me when I need it and lets me go as fast as I want. It doesn't embarrass me."

Some of the top-ranking officers with whom I spoke believe (with me) that the teaching machine can become a basic method of instruction for the military services. It can help young men become more intelligent soldiers and obtain a better grasp of their work.

Because the military services are able to spend huge sums of money, most of the large-scale testing of machines has taken place among military personnel. One thing is certain: the armed forces are already giving the teaching-machine movement its biggest financial boost.

Teaching Machines and Underdeveloped Countries

A UNESCO survey of education revealed that only a little over half the world's school-age children were in school in 1954. The percentage is still considerably worse in many underdeveloped countries. For example:

Ethiopia: of three and a half million people eligible for schooling, only 150,000 are in school.

Philippines: 10 per cent of school-age children never start school; 72 per cent do not finish the sixth grade.

Brazil: 30 per cent do not enter first grade; of those who do only 8 per cent reach fourth grade.

Haiti: one rural child in seven is in elementary school; there are no rural secondary schools.

The United States is rendering educational assistance to many of these countries, of course. A good percentage of the projected 7,000 Peace Corpsmen will serve as teachers in host nations. Under the Fulbright Act, the Smith-Mundt Program, and the State Department Exchange Program, we send roughly $100 million a year overseas for educational purposes. Needless to say, however, both the teachers and the funds amount to a little drop in a huge bucket of ignorance and illiteracy. Moreover, our assistance pretty much follows the methods of the traditional classroom, with its slowness, its failure to adjust to individual students.

The gravity of the problem is recognized. At a recent Washington conference on new learning devices for underdeveloped countries, the following goals came to the fore:

1. The training, in a short time, of large numbers of adults to fill sub-professional jobs from semi-skilled to technical levels.
2. Increasing the numbers of secondary school teachers by inservice upgrading of elementary teachers.
3. Teaching basic job skills and developing enthusiasm toward work with the hands—something the educated cadres of emerging nations tend to look on with disdain.
4. Expanding science education, particularly in elementary and secondary schools and among adults.
5. Increasing adult literacy.
6. Promoting mass education through the mass media.
7. Increasing the number of teachers in English as a second language and improving methods of teaching English.

Such an undertaking is immense and necessary. Money will do a great deal. American teachers can help. Bringing students of other countries to American schools will help. But none of these things, in my estimation, holds as much promise for underdeveloped nations as the teaching machine and programmed learning.

Teaching machines are an obvious remedy for the lack of trained teachers.

Teaching machines are the answer to the most pressing educational demands of all: speed.

Teaching machines are ideal both for educating the masses and responding to the needs of individuals.

Programmed learning has the same psychological validity (that of question-answer, response-reward) for most other cultures as it does for American students.

Now that the teaching machine is coming of age in the

United States I believe we can use it with tremendous effect in the educational systems of underdeveloped nations. At first we could supply machines, programs, and programmed textbooks which would teach the sciences, English, agriculture, machine skills, and other basic subjects in the language of the local country. Concurrently, we might set up technical schools which would instruct local teachers and psychologists in the art of programming. Eventually, of course, the underdeveloped nations would take over complete control of their educational philosophy and materials. But there will be a need for American machines and ideas for many years to come.

This is only the broad outline of what we can do. In introducing machines many problems will face us. What courses should we program first? In multilingual nations, should we program only the main language or the subsidiary ones as well? Should we start with adults or with elementary school children? Should we work in the bigger cities, rural villages, or both simultaneously? Will electricity be available? Which should we emphasize, books or machines? Should we give equal stress to general education and agricultural-technical subjects?

These questions, complicated and difficult as they may be, must be answered. If we don't find the answers the Soviets will. The result will then be catastrophic. We have the opportunity to help our friends. This opportunity must not be neglected.

Teaching machines, to be used by underdeveloped countries to reduce excessively high illiteracy rates, should become our first order of business. Just as we dare not, in today's Cold War spirit, neglect the youth of our country, we dare not neglect the education of the youth of the world.

Nothing can obscure an essential fact: the educational requirements of the 20th century cannot be met with 19th-century techniques. There are just too many people involved, too many political and economic reasons for deliberate speed. The immensity of the task demands bold action: setting up a system of educational aid to underdeveloped countries with the focus on teaching machines and programmed learning.

This bold new approach is essential. It must combine both the mechanical and human elements of our educational technology. Far from dehumanizing the populace, the teaching machine will be a God-send to millions of illiterate children and adults.

Psychologists, educators, statesmen, and scientists working together must evolve a sound educational program designed to eliminate illiteracy. This can be done in large part through our technological developments, including teaching machines and programmed instruction.

CHAPTER SEVEN

Are Administrators Accepting Machines?

However crucial the attitude of children and teachers may be, programmed learning must first be accepted, welcomed, and sought after by administrators if it is to succeed. For this reason I made a survey of 300 school superintendents and state commissioners of education in all parts of the country. Many of the superintendents have either experimented with teaching machines or resolved to do so in the near future. I asked four questions:

(1) Do you plan to introduce programmed learning in your school or school system, and if so, when and under what conditions? If you have already experimented with teaching machines, please indicate the results.

(2) In your opinion, to what extent can teaching machines replace teachers?

(3) Do you believe the machines can help students whose learning ability has been impaired for one reason or another?

(4) Do you think programmed learning is a fad or does it have permanent value?

Question One

Let's take the answers one at a time. First, I learned that about half of the 300 commissioners and superintendents had already used the machines on an experimental basis. Another 25 per cent intended to do so in the near future, while the remaining 25 per cent were adopting a wait-and-see, show-me attitude. Most of the superintendents in the first category had used the machines in one or two classrooms, a few subjects, or one entire grade. I found no school system which had made immediate efforts to supply all its students with machines. Programmed learning must first pass its experimental acid test on a wide scale.

Most of the 150 administrators who have already tried the machines indicated they are pleased with the results. In many instances they have appointed committees of teachers and parents to evaluate the new device; the consensus is that machines pose no super-mechanized threat to the individuality of students but make each student unique.

I found that in this experimental stage the programmed book is more popular than the machine. It costs less and is more manageable for purposes of evaluation. Machines have made their greatest progress in the teaching of languages, where the audio-visual technique has demonstrated its value.

The 75 or so administrators in the show-me category gave a variety of reasons for their position. Many were waiting for more and better programmed material to use in the machines. They were not convinced that the few programs already on the market were of proven worth. Other administrators were skeptical about the whole idea of programmed learning.

"We are not enthusiastic about teaching machines, as some people seem to be," said Dr. George N. Wells, school superintendent in Bloomington, Illinois. "We expect to use this new device as an aid and nothing more."

A similar view was expressed by Dr. Frank B. Decker, commissioner of education for Nebraska: "I have many reservations about teaching machines, just as I have reservations about educational television. I try my best to keep an open mind. I don't want to accept or reject machines simply because they're new."

Apparently nobody's stampeding anybody in that bedrock of Yankee individualism, Vermont. Says Burlington superintendent of schools Allan J. Heath, tersely: "We do not plan to introduce teaching machines or programmed instruction now or within the foreseeable future."

From all the evidence I can presently gather, however, I predict the great majority of school systems in America will introduce teaching machines within the next five years.

Question Two

The second question was: "Can machines replace teachers?" Here it seemed I had waved a bright red flag, and administrators charged at it with an overwhelming "No!" Since most of the typical explanations were offered in a previous chapter, there is no need for great detail here. The consensus was that machines will relieve the teacher of paper work, drillwork, and other assorted drudgeries. They will enable her to devote more time to individual students. They will free her for that essential task in education—the stimulation of ideas. They will probably confront her with bigger classes. But they decidedly will not eliminate her. Only a small minority of the administrators I questioned said they would experiment with machines to see if they could reduce the size of their teaching staffs.

Question Three

To the third question, "Can machines help students who have one or another learning impediment?" again the answer was almost unanimous, and this time it was "Yes." Administrators generally believe that programmed learning will do its best work with gifted or retarded students—the two extremes. As I discovered in my tour of the laboratories in Albuquerque, many emotionally disturbed children regard the machine almost as a personal friend. The machine is particularly helpful for children whose slowness comes not from low intelligence but from poor study habits, insecurity, inability to get along in a group, and other emotional maladjustments. Programmed learning cannot serve as a crutch for these children: after all, they must live in a world of people rather than a laboratory of machines. Nevertheless, teaching machines may give them enough confidence to return to the class group with a good chance of success.

Question Four

The fourth question was: "Is programmed learning a fad or something of permanent value?" The answers fall into roughly the same pattern as that for the first question. Less than 10 per cent of the superintendents and commissioners think programmed learning has no permanent value. About an equal number believe, as I do, that teaching machines represent one of the greatest advances in the history of education. The majority, however, can best be described as cautiously optimistic.

Several points of view characterize this middle-of-the-road group. One is that teaching machines will carry the same weight as other classroom aids such as television, movies, and tape recorders. Many administrators are convinced that programmed learning has a definite but modest role to play, and that this role may be undermined by extravagant claims which can only result in disappointment and frustration. Other administrators believe the success of the whole movement depends on how teachers react to it and how well they are prepared for it. Still others make a distinction between the types of programmed teaching devices. Machines may be a fad, they say, but programmed learning in book form is here to stay.

The hopeful but conservative attitude of these superintendents and commissioners is summed up in the advice given to them by their trade journal, *School Management:* "If you are looking into the possibilities of programmed instruction for your school, let your watchword be: Caution, go slow."

Another conservative, balanced and entirely reasonable summary was given to me by Dr. Thomas G. Pullen, Jr., superintendent of Maryland's department of education. He wrote: "In my 40 years of experience, I have lived through a lot of new ideas—the project method, the Morrisonian Unit, the Dalton Plan, and a host of others. Most of these ideas had some value and while, like the Arab's tents, they have silently stolen away, possibly they have left some vestige of their presence, and some of it has been good.

"The chief value that comes from movements of this kind is that they stimulate thinking and re-evaluation. Of course, in some cases, these things merely confirm us in our reactionary positions, but so long as there is stimulation there is hope. The great danger of all these movements is that they give lay people the idea that here is the one and only true way to learning. We must bear in mind the truth of what Aristotle told Alexander, 'There is no royal road to learning.'

"I should like to add that there are almost as many roads to learning as there are individuals, and the job of the teacher is to discover the way that is best and most effective for each student."

That's good advice. But I would add one proviso: the "wait-and-see, go-slow" caution should not prevent superintendents from making a wholehearted study of programmed learning. If it isn't a royal road, it is still the best path we've yet discovered to a good education.

A Reading Generation

At what level should teaching machines be used? College? High school? Elementary school? Kindergarten?

At all levels!

I watched kindergartners learn to read the machine way. I saw little 4-, 5- and 6-year-olds, of average ability, of their own volition, use the machines, match words, and learn how to spell "boy," "cat," "dog" and other simple words.

Let's forget the controversy over the use of flash cards, see-and-say, or phonics, methods which may be outmoded before the present decade ends. The teaching of reading through the machine method has tremendous potentialities. Traditional ways of teaching reading do not provide a child with proper motivation. The teaching-machine program can help pupils learn to distinguish letters and words. They can be taught to identify letters, and if a phonographic attachment is placed on the machine, pupils can read the printed words and distinguish sounds and phrases. The students are active; they participate.

This, of course, is in marked contrast with classroom instruction or with educational television. If a student in a reading class is ill for a day, is out for two weeks with the measles, has a bad toothache, or doesn't pay attention, he falls behind. The

In this discussion I learned the reactions of a class of Roanoke high school students who took an E.B.F.-Temac algebra program.

teacher may be unable to give the child enough individual instruction to bring him back to the level of his classmates. Also, the immediate and frequent reinforcement that he gets in a programmed machine sustains his interest. He likes what he is doing. He does not daydream. He is usually free from tension.

"He has no reason to be anxious about an impending examination for none is required," said Dr. Skinner. "Both he and his instructor know where he stands at all times."

Much more work will have to be done in the field of programmed instruction. But what I have seen has convinced me that reading can be taught at an early age. We may yet develop a generation of youth who can read. We know that the present methods have not fully succeeded. We should give the teaching machine a chance to show what it can do.

Let's Look at the Budget

When the Egyptians built the pyramids, they used thousands of slaves to pull the huge rocks and slabs. Undoubtedly this was one of the most difficult and inefficient ways to use human beings.

Suppose you had been able to walk over to a Pharaoh and said: "Why are you using human slaves to build these monuments? Why don't you let me supply you with cranes, steam shovels, bulldozers and dynamite? With 100 men and a dozen machines, I can replace the work that is now being done by hundreds of thousands of your human slaves, and with less wear and tear on them, too."

Wouldn't Pharaoh have answered: "Your mighty time-saving and efficient gadgets may be all that you describe. But tell me, will they save me money?"

Some boards of education are saying today: "Why should we buy teaching machines? They're more expensive than teachers."

"I think teaching machines are worthwhile," one superintendent told me, "but I'm not sure I can get my board to buy them. They'll cost a lot of money."

This statement reflects a common concern of educators to whom practice is as important as theory. Without a doubt, teaching machines are going to fatten the budget of any school board. In the short run, at least, they'll be expensive.

When a school decides to buy machines, it will make two kinds of capital outlay: one for the machines themselves and one for the programs. If it buys self-tutoring books, of course, it gets both the program and the program-carrier in one package. However, this latter investment has certain economic disadvantages, as we shall see.

Let's take a look at some costs. The prices of five machines now in use are:

The Min-Max I $20.00
The Min-Max II $25.00
Dyna-Slide's Program Scanner $40.00
The Foringer Teaching Machine $80.00
The Rheem-Califone Machine $157.00
The Western Design Auto-Tutor $5,000.00

What about programmed books? Doubleday puts out the Tutor-Texts (Dr. Crowder's scrambled books) for $3.95. Encyclopaedia Britannica's full-year mathematics course sells for $12.50 up. Grolier is marketing books that range in price from $7.50 to $15.00. Other books cost as little as $2.95.

Programs for machines generally cost between $10 and $15. This is where the greatest expense comes, for while one machine may suffice for ten students, each student must have his own program. Today it costs anywhere from $25,000 to $50,000 to prepare and test one-year high school programs. As more and more schools buy them, however, they will be produced in greater quantity and at less per unit expense.

School boards now face an economic choice: whether to buy the machines and programs at a fairly high cost or the self-tutoring books, which cost less but must be discarded after one student has used them. Some programs for machines must also be discarded after use by a single student. Most machines, however, are designed so that the student writes his answers on a roll of paper separate from the program. The program can thus be used indefinitely. At least one book is also designed without write-ins. In the present experimental stage, most schools are buying the books. It is conceivable that programs for machines will eventually cost less than the books, however, and if this happens it may be less expensive in the long run for schools to buy machines.

Manufacturers of machines, programs, and books have several avenues open to them toward a reduction in costs. One is mass production, which will come about once the new technique is accepted by a majority of American schools. Another is the use of less expensive materials. Some book publishers (Harcourt, Brace & World, for one) have issued self-tutoring texts as paperbacks, hoping that they will attract a mass market for programmed learning, while others (such as McGraw-Hill) are issuing technical programmed books in paperback, but at prices just below hard-cover prices.

A third avenue, already being explored by Grolier, is the manufacture of programs which can be used in book form or in machines. In one case the material is bound and jacketed, while in the other it is loose-leaf and can be picked up in single sheets. Designing a single machine to serve 30 or so pupils simultaneously would be a fourth economizing step. Such a device might be centrally controlled with small extensions on each table or desk—much like using several deployed screens for one television receiver. As a result of these various methods of cost-cutting, machines may soon be on the market for half the current prices. Several companies have already blueprinted machines that will sell for as little as $5.00.

When a school board decides to order machines, it, too, can economize. Since machines can be used at different times of the day by different students, it would be a good idea to buy those machines for which there is the greatest variety of programs.

One school board in the Midwest learned this lesson the hard way. After buying 20 machines for $5,000 each—a nice fat $100,000 investment—it discovered that no programs had yet been developed for its particular model. Today the 20 machines repose silently in the school's basement; you can buy them just for the cost of hauling them away.

This situation can best be compared to the confusion that existed until recently in the phonograph industry when the market was flooded with the 33-, 45- and 78-speed records. The owner of a machine found he could play only one of the three. He was faced with the dismal prospect of buying three different machines. The manufacturers changed that. Machines today take all three types.

We find that the teaching-machine manufacturers have given us nearly 100 different types. The records—or programs—for them are not interchangeable. They should be.

Other money-saving tactics will become common as programmed instruction gains a foothold. Schools will learn how to schedule a few machines for use by many students in many courses. Classrooms may be built with expanding walls to accommodate the greatly fluctuating class sizes that will come with programmed learning. But the greatest and most sustained economy of all may lie in the amount of time it takes to educate any one student.

Our national education now costs us $20 billion a year. Two related facts bear a large responsibility for the total: it costs roughly $500 a year to educate each child, and it takes 12 years for the great majority of our students to go from first grade through high school. If we could send our children through high school in eleven, ten, or nine years, we would save millions of dollars. Programmed learning may enable us to do just that. (Remember the medical terminology course at Point Park Junior College—see page 76.) Every survey and experiment in the field so far indicates that students—bright, average, or dull—learn faster on a teaching machine than in the classroom.

Not only would quicker schooling be less expensive (provided of course that it didn't sacrifice quality, or that the cost of machines didn't outweigh the value of the time saved), but it would also strengthen our economy by turning students into productive citizens at an earlier age than heretofore. This is a long-term and fairly incalculable profit. In the meantime we must expect programmed learning to increase the costs of our school budgets.

What, then, can administrators expect from a swollen budget caused by installation of a teaching-machine system? I will summarize the advantages this way:

1. Through individual instruction, brighter children will be able to advance faster, and the others go at their own pace.

2. The teacher will be freed of much routine work, and thus be able to do more creative teaching.

3. Teaching techniques will improve, since the teachers will get the best scientific and educational approach to learning.

We should invest what we can afford in machines and programmed instruction.

Machines, books, and programs are still expensive, and a lot of money will have to be devoted to the retraining of teachers. Thus, every school board must juggle immediate expense against eventual returns and ask: "Is programmed learning worth it?"

My own answer is "Yes," but not for strictly economic reasons. As a matter of fact, the cost of education is ultimately not half so crucial as the service it performs. Education strengthens our democracy just as much as national defense preserves it; both are beyond mere questions of budget-balancing. If programmed learning can improve our education, we should not begrudge its expense.

Admittedly, a technique that augurs broad changes will meet

broad resistance. It is a curious fact that man is forever moving ahead but looking backward. He always refers to "the good old days." Even Socrates talked about the good old days when children knew how to obey their parents.

Truthfully, we should admit that the good old days in education weren't really that good. At any rate the age of the machine has come. It may be a costly machine, but on the other hand it may help our children become wiser men and women and it may help us value and safeguard the things we believe in.

Look at the budget? Yes. But let's also look at our children. Teaching machines can pay human dividends.

CHAPTER EIGHT

Challenges Ahead

It may be clear to the reader at this point that I'm optimistic about teaching machines. I think they're here to stay, and I believe their contributions to American education can be predicted with reasonable accuracy.

As we have seen, these contributions will be:

(1) Responsiveness to individual differences. Machines will enable almost all students to learn at a rate commensurate with their intelligence, without wasting time repeating material they are already familiar with.

(2) A feed-back system of reinforcements and rewards. This encourages almost all students to do their best.

(3) An antidote to the aversive psychology of most present-day classrooms. Programmed learning is enjoyable.

(4) Special values in machines for gifted students and remedial instruction, as well as for those who are physically or mentally retarded or emotionally disturbed.

(5) A vast improvement in the teaching of tool subjects like

science, mathematics, and language, and a significant, if lesser, improvement in subjects like history and literature.

(6) A reduction in the amount of routine teaching drudgery, drill and paper work that now takes up so much of a teacher's time, and a consequent release of time for individual problems, group discussions, conferences, and curriculum development. This will enhance the teacher's prestige.

(7) A tremendous boost to education outside of the classroom: in underdeveloped countries, rural areas, industry, the armed forces, and home study courses.

A decade will probably come and go before these achievements can be demonstrated as fact, however. In the meantime, programmed learning will have to overcome numerous challenges to its philosophy and practice. If these challenges are not met, teaching machines may never develop further than educational television, which promised so much and has delivered so little.

What are the problems that lie ahead? I believe they can be designated as: problems of cultural inertia, of administration, and of programmed learning itself. As we shall see, they all have some relation to one another and must be attacked at their common roots, which reach into the nature and making of programs.

Cultural Inertia

Dr. Skinner puts the first problem bluntly: "The necessary techniques for a renaissance in education are known. The necessary equipment can be produced. We have the skills, the brains, and the know-how to meet the challenge. Nothing stands in the way," he says, "but cultural inertia."

It is an oddity of American culture that a society which has developed the most advanced machines in the world is also the most uncomfortable in their presence. We view them as threats to our individuality, our flesh-and-blood humanity, and to our standing among the intellectual nations of this world. That next new analog computer—we feel deep down in our bones—is going to outwit us all and make us all its slaves. Consequently, we hope it won't work, or at least not too well.

The story is told that when Robert Fulton built his steamboat, a group of "razzers" stood on the banks of Lake Erie as the monster without sails was about to make way. "It won't go, it won't go, it won't go," they chanted.

Slowly the engine began to turn over, and the world's first steamboat, hissing like a mad dragon, swung out into the lake. Immediately, without missing a beat, the terrified watchers cried: "It won't stop! It won't stop! It won't stop!"

That is the way many teaching machine critics react. Some of them secretly hope it won't work, while others are afraid that, like an aroused Frankenstein, it won't stop. Why this irrational response? The answer, I believe, is that at a level of mind beyond logic, these people feel teaching machines are a threat to our children—and a *dehumanizing* threat. More than once I have heard parents express the fear that machines would in some vague way "mechanize" students and rob them of independence.

This response has greeted many new technological advances. When people are robbed of their humanity, the robbing has either been done by other people or by themselves, but never really by machines. Still, we *are* faced with the existence of an anti-teaching-machine bias among some parents. Just what its impact on the new movement will be, I can't say. I do know manufacturers and educators will have to convince the American public that machines are worthwhile, for education is a public concern and programmed learning will affect everybody.

The Frankenstein myth is the most irrational of all problems now confronting the teaching-machine movement. It is not the most difficult, however. Without a doubt the biggest challenge will be to enlist the cooperation of the majority of our teachers.

In my conversations with teachers, I found many who were hostile to programmed learning. The simplest expression of this hostility was an unwillingness to change career-long methods of teaching. Like everybody else, teachers are creatures of habit.

Other teachers still regard a machine as a cross between a crackpot idea and a radical school innovation, despite the fact that experiments are going on in 500 of the nation's high schools.

Some teachers are afraid the machines will give them more, rather than less, work. They point to the enormous amount of work needed to correct the frequent tests given in connection with programmed instruction. With just 30 children in a class but perhaps 15 different levels of instruction, the teacher may be called upon to do more individualized work than she now does.

Many teachers are not convinced that the psychological basis of programmed instruction is sound. They believe that students should get an over-all program and not take the subjects in small doses. Teachers are particularly concerned lest the creative child be bored with the teaching machine.

Some distrust machines because, by encouraging individual rates of learning, they may make class discipline more difficult. As I have suggested earlier, we may need a new kind of grade and class structure to handle programmed learning. This might solve the problem of discipline, but it raises the most emotion-fraught questions of all: Where will the teacher fit into the new structure? To what extent (particularly in the tool subjects) will she be replaced? Until teachers are assured they will have an

In this crowded Chicago elementary school classroom, the Min-Max II is being used by every student.

honorable place in programmed learning, many of them will continue to view it with apprehension and downright hostility. Thus the remark of one teacher to me: "Why should I be a guinea pig for this contraption? If it works, I might be out of a job."

Like many criticisms of teaching machines, this one is based on insufficient information, which is based in turn on a lack of adequate research. But, if most examples of resistance to the new technique can be traced to inconclusive research, so can many instances of undue optimism. There is a danger that the "oversell" now taking place could boomerang.

Overselling the New Program

"The public may first achieve high enthusiasm and then disillusionment," says Dean Keppel. "Five years ago educational television was considered the greatest boon education ever had. Neither television nor the teaching machine will replace the book, the basic instrument for learning. If disillusionment with machines comes, people may lose sight of the strength that does exist in programmed instruction."

Thus, in terms of a broad, popular acceptance of teaching machines, there are two resisting elements: people who distrust the machine itself, and teachers who are worried about its effect on their profession and their careers. Further research should solve one problem; research and careful administrative planning may solve the other.

One thing is certain: the teacher cannot move forward unless the administrator backs her up. And one thing is encouraging: in schools throughout the country where teaching machines have been introduced, the superintendent or principal has been the spearhead of progress. Administrators and educational groups that represent the teaching profession have shown an amazing desire to take part in the movement; amazing, because as a rule these authorities are the last to accept technological advances; amazing also because several problems and dilemmas have now emerged at the administrative level of programmed learning.

One problem I mentioned earlier was: "Is it wiser to invest now in machines or programmed books?" We might also ask whether and when the $1,000 machine would be more advantageous than the $20 model. Of course there is the huge problem of classroom organization, which must be tackled at or before beginning any investment in programmed learning.

Furthermore, the tremendous variety of machines now in existence is not only an educational goldmine; it is an embarrassment of riches. Unfortunately programs used in these machines cannot be interchanged. What fits into the Min-Max, for instance, doesn't fit into the Auto-Tutor. As a result, superintendents who find that Program X is the best there is in music and Program Y the best in history will either have to buy two kinds of machines or compromise on one of the programs. This dilemma will persist until there is a full range of good material for every machine or the machines can take any style of program. The 300-odd programs in existence today are a tiny fraction of the number we will ultimately need.

Central Clearing House

Underlying these administrative problems is the necessity for, and lack of, a central clearing house for programmed learning. Such an agency would evaluate and recommend programs, machines, and books. It would help superintendents decide which program was a good investment and which was not, which grade reorganization scheme was sound and which would only add to the confusion. Perhaps an agency for programmed learning could be set up by the National Education Association or the U.S. Office of Education. At any rate, the need for one is great and immediate.

This requirement suggests the root of all problems in the teaching machine movement: the lack of a firm consensus about programs. Thus the cautionary remarks of *School Management:* "While teaching machines have been tested on students in laboratory experiments in a handful of schools and colleges, almost no such testing has been done in realistic conditions in elementary or secondary schools."

Because there hasn't been time for thorough research into some aspects of programmed learning, and because different theories about it are partially unresolved, the whole movement seems to be moving ahead in scatter-shot fashion. Maybe this is inevitable in a young movement; it might even be healthy. But sooner or later a broad consensus will have to develop or competition will become chaos.

The greatest success of the teaching machines so far has been to teach children facts necessary to understand a subject.

But, programs in the social studies probably can be worked out to help the student develop self-dependence in learning, and a deep interest in the events of the day. An important aim of the social studies program should be to develop within the students a capacity to understand the new political, economic and social problems of the current scene. In the programmed learning situation, a student must develop appreciation and reflective thinking.

Can such complexities be put into machine form? Can we create attitudes? Can we develop appreciation? Can we instill the ability to interpret? Can creativity be taught?

We don't know. But research teams are exploring these fields. Time alone, plus massive field experiments, will tell.

Unsettled Questions

Where are the areas of disagreement, incomplete knowledge, and confusion? What are some of the hazards? The following list won't give all the answers, but I do think it covers the main points.

1. There is still an unsettled controversy about the basic structure of programmed learning. Should learning be as errorless as possible, or can it profit from a certain amount of

mistakes? Should all responses be constructed by the student, or will he learn just as well through multiple-choice selection? By breaking instruction down into very small steps, will we produce logical thinkers or unimaginative ones who are unable to grasp broad ideas in their entirety? Does immediate reinforcement strengthen learning or rob it of discipline? Finally, is a student really "engaged" in the learning process when he is limited to making one-word or one-sentence answers, or when all he does is push a button?

Admittedly, stating the problem in either form may distort and oversimplify it a little, but I think the reader can now grasp some of its major elements. Many of the questions—and especially the last one—might be answered by allowing students to write longer responses to programmed questions. While this would mean more work for programmers and teachers, it would broaden the base of a somewhat narrow technique.

2. A second difference of opinion is concerned with programmed learning's versatility. How accurate is Mr. Waller in saying that composition can be taught? Or Dr. Homme in saying that Shakespeare can be taught? Or Dr. Skinner in saying anything that can be verbalized can be taught? Or other authorities in saying that only the basic tool subjects can be taught?

3. The degree to which a student retains programmed learning is still uncertain.

4. Isn't it important for a student to have broad and persistent interrelationships with his classmates and teachers? Do machines tend to insulate each child in his own private little world?

5. Some children appear to have a natural hostility toward machines. They may be simply allergic to electronic devices.

6. In a recent study of slums and slum children, Dr. James B. Conant, former president of Harvard, points out that many underprivileged youngsters do not respond to the kind of reinforcement they get in programmed learning. "What's so good about being right?" they seem to ask. "Where has being right ever got me or my brothers and sisters?" Though this attitude isn't verbalized, it does exist, and it represents a lack of the kind of motivation which teaching machines presuppose.

7. How many hours a day can a student cope with programmed instruction? Doesn't it become too monotonous, too facile, too reflexive after a certain period? Perhaps no more than two hours in a normal six-hour school day should be devoted to machines. Homework might also be assigned in programmed form.

8. Granting there is room for a teacher in all programmed courses, her usefulness may still be impaired. If she finds certain areas of the program not to her liking, she'll have to use them anyway. The reason for this is that any question in a program can be understood only in relation to preceding questions; none can be omitted. Yet, a good teacher should enliven a course with her own point of view. She should not be tied down to teaching precisely what someone in a distant laboratory has written out.

9. Cheating will be a problem with most programmed books. Dr. Homme has said programmed learning will outmode dishonesty, but some students don't take their education seriously enough to have the patience even for step-by-step study. They will merely work from frame to frame, looking ahead for answers whenever they choose.

Problems of Programming

The next two problems deal not with the nature or psychology of programmed learning, but with the subject-matter that goes into it, and with the people who formulate it. These problems are very important, and I will treat them in greater detail than the others.

10. Antedating the teaching machine, and perhaps equal to it in importance, is a profound reshaping of the content of many courses, especially in history, grammar, the sciences, and mathematics. Yale is now working on an improved math curriculum, M.I.T. on physics, University of Chicago on history, the University of Illinois on arithmetic, Harvard on psychology, chemistry, and foreign languages. This undertaking is absolutely vital, for in many places curricula are still found which are almost medieval in content. Thus we have Dr. Howard F. Fehr of the Columbia University math department saying: "Any 17th-century mathematician reappearing upon earth today could enter most classrooms in our traditional high school and without any preparation, teach the present curriculum, so far is it behind the times."

Will the new programmed books and machines take advantage of the new curricula? Will they teach better programs or will they merely teach better?

In the main, programs now emerging from various laboratories are simply a rehash of existing textbooks. This is one of the few serious failings of programmed learning today, a failing despite the assurances of Harvard's Dean Keppel: "Our concern is that high quality be at the core of the teaching machine curriculum rather than any effort to show that we can save time;" and of Mr. Waller: "We do not intend to perpetuate the poor programs found in existing curricula. We will spare no expense to develop a program that will meet the highest standards of our educational system."

It is this very expense that is leading most program manufacturers down the worn path of old curricula. A good program today can cost as much as $75,000. Few programmers are willing to risk investments of that size on courses which are so controversial or so new that *as courses* they must fight for a market. Few school boards are willing to invest thousands of dollars in a machine for a program which hasn't already demonstrated its worth. For the last 30 or 40 years, education has been one of the most conservative industries in America.

There are, however, some hopeful signs. A few manufacturers seem to be willing to risk capital on the latest curricula. One of the best jobs in this regard is being done by the Center for Programed Instruction, whose budget is given regular transfusions by the Carnegie Corporation. At present the Center is readying courses in French, German, Latin, junior and senior college mathematics, English, spelling, reading, vocabulary building, social science, chemistry, and physics. These courses will have the most advanced curricula now available.

The Center is a special case, however, for most other programmers are playing it safe with standard curricula. More's the pity. In the midst of a technological revolution which most schools and colleges are ready to encourage, it would be a shame to find that we have a beautiful machine, well painted and designed, but housing a McGuffey-type reader.

11. The final problem in this series is the competence of programmers now at work around the country. Here is a brief conversation I had with a young college graduate who was programming a text in chemistry:

"Have you ever written a textbook before?"
"No."

"How are you going about this programming?"

"I use my college notes quite a bit. You see, I took chemistry in college, so I refer to my books and notes to make certain what I'm writing down is correct."

This young lady may develop into an excellent programmer in time, but I don't know if the program she's designing now should be used extensively until it has been thoroughly examined by subject specialists.

Another conversation with a young college graduate who was working on a program in electricity for the Navy:

"What made you decide to become a programmer?"

"Frankly, I think it's interesting. Actually, I needed a job."

Many other programmers I talked to had little experience in education. They had even less experience with the specialized form of education which is programmed learning. In every instance, of course, their work was backed up by competent psychologists and tested on students. Furthermore, they represented a minority of the programmers now writing for manufacturers; most of their co-workers had enough experience to handle their jobs adequately.

Nevertheless, the existence of even a small group of untrained programmers is cause for alarm. One authority who *is* alarmed is Dr. Holland, the Harvard psychologist and colleague of Dr. Skinner. Disturbed by the ease with which amateurs were finding work as programmers, he made this sharp comment: "The ill-advised efforts of some of our friends who prepare courses for machines without using the right techniques may bury the whole movement in a great wave of teaching-machine tapes."

Now, lest I close on a note of pessimism which is not at all my conviction, I must say that I have just listed eleven problems which I thoroughly believe will be solved. Serious as some of them are, they are outweighed massively by the contributions that programmed learning can make to our system of education. These contributions, summarized at the beginning of this chapter and treated in some detail elsewhere in the book, do not need to be repeated here. Briefly, then, I want to assure the reader of an opinion of mine which, because it wasn't central to this book, may not have been surmised:

The American system of education is the best there is. Its traditions are good.

And:

Programmed learning is new. Its worth is untested. Machines are still regarded as curiosities.

But:

The future belongs to those who are willing to experiment.

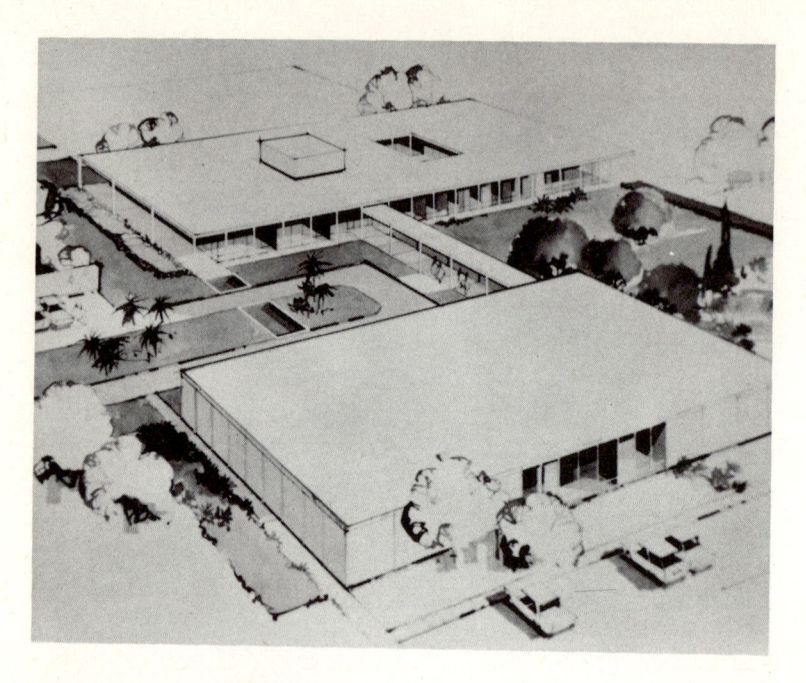

New facilities are being built at Stanford Industrial Park, Palo Alto, California, to house the Britannica Center for Studies in Learning and Motivation. This is the architect's drawing of the building in which programmed learning materials will be created and tested.

CHAPTER NINE

Research Findings

It is estimated that some $25 million a year is spent on research in programmed learning. In 1957 eight known projects were underway; in 1959, sixty; in 1961, over 100; and this year, over 200. Unmistakably, the boom is on.

The effects of this research won't be fully known for another five to ten years. In my own observations of 100 finished experiments, however, I became convinced of one truth: Everybody can learn with teaching machines—students of all ages, adults, factory workers, military personnel.

Research centers for programmed instruction exist in Albuquerque with Teaching Materials, Inc.; in Pittsburgh with the American Institute; in Palo Alto with Encyclopaedia Britannica Films; in New York with the Center for Programed Instruction and with Basic Systems; in Santa Monica with the United States Industries and with the Systems Development Corp.; in London with Systems Research Ltd. (under the sponsorship of the European office of the U.S. Air Force Research and Development Command).

Many of the leading colleges of the nation are conducting experiments. Among them are Harvard, Hamilton, Stanford, Dartmouth, Oberlin, Ohio State. The research subjects are algebra, spelling, electronics, psychology, languages, logic, statistics, reading, music, religion, and many others. The questions they are considering are: What subjects can be taught? How much time should students spend each day on machines? What is the role of the teacher? What makes programmed learning effective? Let's hope that these studies will not become too involved or too technical.

I won't attempt a broad grasp of what all the research done so far means, especially since other chapters have dealt with this in a direct way. Rather, let me give you the basic findings obtained thus far, in capsulized form:

● Harvard's Douglas Porter finds that spelling can be taught more effectively by machine than by traditional methods.

● Machines have proven to be very adaptable to tying-in with other mechanical devices such as television, radio, motion pictures, and tape recorders.

● One study revealed that 51 per cent of the students using the machines got A's in contrast to 10 per cent in the control group.

● Machines are very effective with bright children, with the deaf, and with children who are mentally retarded or emotionally disturbed.

● Machines reduce the gap between slow and bright student. The United States Office of Education reports: "The tendency is for students with lower ability to achieve more and thereby become more like the high-ability students in performance."

• A Harvard study suggests: the smaller the steps in a program, the more the learning and the greater the time it takes to learn it. Also: there is little difference in efficiency between constructed-response programs and multiple-choice programs.

• At Hamilton College, the average grade in a freshman logic course jumped 30 points after programmed instruction was introduced.

These are only a few of the findings. These and others have been discussed in greater detail elsewhere in the book.

The most important research job ahead is to perfect both the machine and the programmed instruction.

We need a two-pronged study. More research in the basic concepts of learning and teaching machine principles is not enough. The second attack should be a massive field experiment. Even the Roanoke experiment only reached 1,000 students. Why not an experiment now to reach 100,000? or 500,000?

For the reader who has a working interest in the latest developments in teaching-machine research, the following list of current research and programming projects may prove helpful:

Colleges and Universities:

Alabama University: a program to improve study habits in college students.

Bucknell University: research into mathematics for superior high school students.

Calabrese School, Denver: reading instruction for retarded children.

University of California: elementary science, reading, and mathematics.

Carnegie Institute of Technology: engineering for university students.

Dartmouth University Medical School: entire first two-year curriculum for medical students; programs in anatomy, biochemistry, microbiology, pathology, pharmacology, and physiology.

Devereux School, Devon, Pa.: programs for low-I.Q. children.

Earlham College: music, freshman English, Russian, the Old Testament.

Hamilton College: logic.

Harvard University: spelling for the second, fourth and sixth grades; elementary math, reading, grammar, French, and Mandarin Chinese.

Hollins College: various projects for Encyclopaedia Britannica Films.

University of Houston: remedial English.

University of Illinois: specialized education areas.

Indiana University: elementary Russian.

University of Maryland: speech therapy, programs for aphasics.

University of Michigan: self-instruction in languages.

University of Nevada: problem-solving.

University of Pittsburgh: programs for the American Institute for Research.

Point Park Junior College, Pittsburgh: medical secretarial work.

Princeton University: linear equations and binary numbers.

University of Southern California: clearing-house functions under a National Education Association grant. Information available to teachers, administrators.

University of Tennessee: freshman elementary accounting.

Utah State University: college spelling.
University of Virginia: sixth-grade math.

Business and Other Private Organizations:
Bell Telephone: basic electronics for employees.
Britannica Center for Studies in Learning and Motivation (Stanford University): wide range of programs.
Doubleday and Co.: wide range of programmed texts.
Electronic Teaching Laboratories, Washington, D.C.: speech therapy.
Systems Development Corp, Santa Monica: value of programmed learning.
Teaching Machines, Inc., Albuquerque: wide range of programs.

Military Services:
Wright-Patterson Air Force Base, Ohio: pilot training, retention of in-flight information.
Also: Air Force Personnel and Training Research Center at Lackland AFB, Texas; Lory AFB, Denver; Randolph AFB, Texas; Goodfellow AFB, Texas.
And: U.S. Army Signal School, Ft. Monmouth, N.J.; U.S. Army Southeastern Signal Corps School, Ft. Gordon, Ga.; Human Resources Research Office, Ft. Benning, Ga.
And: U.S. Naval Training Devices Research Center, Ft. Washington, N.J.; punchboard machines, code instruction.

INDEX

Adult education, 66, 126
Administrators', reactions, 139-151
"Adventures in Algebra," 35, 67
Albuquerque, experiments, 22, 24, 28, *51*, 56, 73, 81, 98, 121
Algebra, experiments, *33*, 35, *39*, 42, 62, *65*, *69*, 73, 81, *82*, 83, 93, 100, *145*
Altronic Tutor, 41
Astra Auto-Score, 31
Audio machines, 27, 40, 41, 122, 131, 148, 168
Audio-visual aids, 27, 38, 41, 131, 133, 140, 142, 168
AutoTutor, *36*, 158
Aversive practices, 91
AVTA machine, 41

Bell, Dr. Genevieve, 57, 77
Book
 programmed, 32, 62, *63*, 147
 sample pages, *34*, *61*, *63*, *65*, *69*, *74*, *76*, *78*, *79*, *125*
 scrambled (nonconsecutive), 35, *36*, 68, *69*, 106, 147
 versus machines, 62
Budget, 146

Calculus, 98, 133
Carnegie Corporation, 23, 50, 129, 163
Central Clearing House, 158
Challenges ahead, 152-165
Cheating, 63, 97, 110, 161
Chemistry, *51*

Class organization, programmed, 114
Course content, 162
Crowder, Norman A., 35, 67, 106
Cultural inertia, 153

Dyna-Slide's Program Scanner, 147

Encyclopaedia Britannica Films, 56, 58, 67, 75, 110, *125*, 147, *166*
English, 71, 87, 95, 104, 137
"English 2600," 33, *34*, 68, 75, 104

Finn, Dr. James D., and Perrin, Dr. Donald G., 43
Foringer Teaching Machine, 147

Geography, experiments, 59
Geometry, experiments, 66, *67*, 73, *74*, 86, 91
German, experiments, 122

Harvard University, experiments, 23, 39, 46, 59, 80, 85, 121, 123, 169
Hill, Larry, 21, 22, 81, 82
History, teaching machines, 37
Home economics, 126
Homme, Dr. Lloyd, 57, *59*, 64, 89, 161
Humanities, 101, 108, 115, 120, 126

173

Industry, response, 66, 126, 130, 171

Job skills, 129, 130, 136

Keppel, Dr. Francis, 103, 119, 157, 162

Languages, 109, 122, 129, 140. See also specific language.
Liberal arts. See Humanities.
Lou Ellen, 24

Mathematics, 36, 67, 87, 99, 109. See also specific subject.
Medical technology class, 21, 57, 76, 149
MemoTutor, 30, 122
Military response, 66, 171
Min-Max I, 18, 25, 28, 29, 31, 41, 77, 82, 84, 108, 147, 158
Min-Max II, 40, 41, 100, 156
Multiple-choice, 27, 35, 38, 63, 68
Music, 124

National defense, teaching machines and, 133
National Education Association, 42, 43, 158
  survey, 44
Nonconsecutive text. See Book, scrambled.

Ohio State University, experiments, 23, 37, 73
Overselling the new program, 157

Perrin, Dr. Donald G., and Finn, Dr. James D., 43
Pigeons, 45
Point Park Junior College, 21, 57, 76, 77, 149
Predictions, 152
Pressey Drum Tutor, 37
Programmed book. See Book.
Programmed instruction, 21, 55
Programmed learning, 45-70
  assets, 53
  class organization, 114, 155
  drawbacks, 133, 159
  overselling, 157
  steps in, 52
Programmed Logic for Automatic Teaching Operations (P.L.A.T.O.), 42
Programming, problems of, 162
Programs and programmers, 55
Psychomotor skills, 40

Questions
  of administrators, 139
  of teachers, 109
  unsettled, 158

Research findings, 167-171
Reactions to teaching machines
  administrators', 139-151
  industry, 66, 126, 130, 171
  military, 66, 171. See also National Defense.
  students', 71-101
  teachers', 102-118, 155
  underdeveloped countries, 135
Reading skills, 77, 121, 144
Rheem-Califone Machine, 147

Roanoke, experiments, 21, 56, 78, 81, 83, *97*, 106, *145*
Rockville Centre, experiments, 62, 63, *64*, 73, 83, 104
Russian, basic, 29, 43

Science, 109, 123
Scrambled book. *See* Book.
Skills
    job, 129, 130, 136
    psychomotor, 40
    reading, 77, 121, 144
    spelling, *63*, 85, 88, 121
Skinner, Dr. B. F., 39, 45, 48, 54, 57, 59, 68, 89, 91, 105, 119, 145, 153
Speech Auto-Instruction Device (S.A.I.D.), 41
"Spelling Self-Taught," 62, *63*
Spelling skills, *63, 78*, 85, 88, 122
Stein, Gertrude, 45
Students, 149, 152, 168
    adult, 66, 126
    average, 83
    below-average, 85
    bright, 79
    emotionally disturbed, 85
    response of, 71-101
Subjects, 114, 119-138, 152
    assorted, 124, 126
    English, 71, 87, 95, 104, 136
    geography, 59
    humanities, 101, 108, 115, 120, 126
    languages, 109, 122, 129, 140. *See also* specific language.
    mathematics, 87, 99, 109. *See also* specific subject.
    music, 124
    reading, 77, 121, 144
    science, 109, 123
    speech, 41
    spelling, *63, 78*, 85, 88, 121
    tool, 108, 120, 155
    vocabulary, 42, 88
Sullivan, Dr. Maurice W., 106, 114, 119
Suggestions for the future, 129

Teacher response, 102-118, 155
    retraining, 110
    shortage, solving the, 112, 135
Teaching machines. *See also* Reactions.
    adult education, 66, 126
    advantages, 136, 150, 152
        over programmed books, 62
    challenges to, 152-165
    common characteristics, 20, 41
    cost, 146, 157
    definition, 43
    flaws, 110, 159
    history, 37
    types
        Altronic Tutor, 41
        Astro Auto-Score, 31
        AutoTutor, *36*, 158
        AVTA Machine, 41
        Dyna-Slide's Program Scanner, 147
        Foringer Teaching Machine, 147
        MemoTutor, *30, 122*
        Min-Max I, *18, 25*, 28, *29*, 31, 41, 77, *82, 84, 108*, 147, 158
        Min-Max II, *40*, 41, 100, *156*
        Pressey Drum Tutor, 37
        Programmed Logic for Automatic Teaching Operation, 42

Rheem-Califone Machine, 147
Speech Auto-Instruction Device, 41
Univox, *32*
Western Auto-Tutor, 31, 147
Wyckoff Film Tutor, 41, 77
Underdeveloped countries, 135
Teaching Machines, Inc., laboratories, 28, 56, *59, 113,* 124
Temac, *33, 39, 64, 65, 74,* 83, 100, *145*
Terminology, 43
Thermodynamics, elements of, 27
Terrace, Herbert S., 46, 55
Tests, 86, 89, 99
Thorndike, Edward L., 37
Time savings, 73, 126, 136, 150
Tool subjects, 108, 120, 155
Turin, experiments, 66, *67*

Underdeveloped countries, teaching machines and, 135
United States Office of Education, 23, 42, 43, 129, 158, 168
University of Illinois, experiments, 42
Univox, *32*
Unsettled questions, 158

Videosonic, 131
Vigorous debate, 106
Vocabulary, 42, 88

Waller, Theodore, 19, 54, 117, 120, 162
Western Auto-Tutor, 31, 147
Wyckoff Film Tutor, 41, 77